The Wisdom of
KARL MARX

The Wisdom of

KARL MARX

PHILOSOPHICAL
LIBRARY

CITADEL PRESS
Kensington Publishing Corp.
www.kensingtonbooks.com

CITADEL PRESS books are published by

Kensington Publishing Corp.
850 Third Avenue
New York, NY 10022.

All Kensington titles, imprints, and distributed lines are available at special quantity discounts for bulk purchases for sales promotions, premiums, fund raising, educational, or institutional use. Special book excerpts or customized printings can also be created to fit specific needs. For details, write or phone the office of the Kensington special sales manager: Kensington Publishing Corp., 850 Third Avenue, New York, NY 10022, attn: Special Sales Department, phone 1-800-221-2647.

First Citadel printing: March 2002

10   9   8   7   6   5   4   3   2   1

Printed in the United States of America

Cataloging data for this title may be obtained from the Library of Congress.

ISBN 0-8065-2329-8

Foreword

Karl Marx was born in Trier, Germany, in 1818 and died in London in 1883. During his later years he became an important social philosopher and a radical political leader, and is renowned today as the father of modern communism.

The son of a jurist, Marx had originally intended to follow his father's profession, but his study of law was terminated by a growing interest in philosophy. He finally decided to devote all his time to philosophy and took a Ph.D. degree in 1842. Shortly thereafter he became editor of a radical newspaper. This paper was suppressed by the German government, and in 1843 Marx left Germany to settle in Paris. It was here that he encountered Friedrich Engels, who was to be his life-long friend and patron. Having become a confirmed socialist, Marx published, in 1848 and with the aid of Engels, the famous *Communist Manifesto*, in which he set forth the basic tenets of his radical philosophy. Returning to Germany in 1848 in order to participate in revolutionary movements there, he met with official disapproval and was forced to flee the country after two years. He found exile in London in 1850 and remained in the British capital for the rest of his life, existing most of the time in dire circumstances, and supporting himself with odd journalistic assignments as well as with the occasional financial contributions of Engels. In 1867 he published the first volume of his monumental work *DAS KAPITAL*, which was eventually to change the shape of the world.

DAS KAPITAL, subsequently published in three volumes, has exerted an enormous influence on the modern world. Marx combined a powerful and profound mind with a capacity for inexhaustible research and study. He made himself thoroughly familiar with all traditional and contemporary economic philosophies, and used this knowledge as a frame of reference for his study of the British economic system. As a result of his disenchantment with the conditions that existed in his time in England, he repudiated all existing socialistic theories as either utopian or unsocialistic and developed a dynamic theory of social change which became the basis of *scientific socialism* and *dialectical materialism.* It is from these that most forms of socialism and communism are derived today.

Objective critics have tended to consider Marx as one of the greatest of economic theorists, one whose views cannot be lightly discounted, but whose system, like all systems, is seriously hampered by its rigidly doctrinaire nature.

MORRIS STOCKHAMMER

LIST OF ABBREVIATIONS

C.	*Capital* (1, 2, 3, 4)
C. C.	*Contribution to the Critique of Hegel's Philosophy of Right*
C. M.	*Communist Manifesto*
C. W.	*Civil War in France*
D. E.	*Differences between the Philosophy of Democritus and the Philosophy of Epicurus*
D. T.	Articles in the N. Y. *Daily Tribune*
E. B.	*The Eighteenth Brumaire of Louis Bonaparte*
G. I.	*German Ideology*
H. F.	*Holy Family*
H. P.	*Demonstration in Hyde Park*
I. Q.	*The Indian Question*
J. Q.	*Papers on the "Jewish Question"*
L. A.	Leading Article of No. 179 of *Koelnische Zeitung*
M.	Manuscripts of 1844
P. E.	*A Contribution to the Critique of Political Economy*
P. P.	*Poverty of Philosophy*
T. F.	*Theses on Feuerbach*

All references are made to Karl Marx's Works "Gesamtausgabe" and to their translations by Moore and Aveling.

The Wisdom of
KARL MARX

A

ABOLITION OF PROPERTY
The abolition of existing (private) property relations is not at all a distinctive feature of communism. . . . The distinguishing feature of communism is the abolition of bourgeois (private) property.—C. M.

ABSOLUTE KNOWLEDGE
Mind, this thinking returning home to its own point of origin—the thinking which, as the anthropological, phenomenological, psychological, ethical, artistic and religious mind is not valid for itself, until ultimately it finds itself, and relates itself to itself, as absolute knowledge in the hence absolute, i.e., abstract mind, and so receives its conscious embodiment in a mode of being corresponding to it.—M.

ABSOLUTE SURPLUS-VALUE
The surplus-value produced by prolongation of the working day, I call absolute surplus-value.—C. 1.

ABSORPTION OF LABOR
The means of production are at once changed into means of

absorption of the labor of others. It is now no longer the laborer that employs the means of production, but the means of production that employ the laborer. Instead of being consumed by him as material elements of his productive activity, they consume him as the ferment necessary to their own life-process, and the life-process of capital consists only in its movement as value constantly expanding, constantly multiplying itself.—C. 1.

ANTAGONISM, SOCIOLOGICAL
The bourgeois relations of production are the last antagonistic form of the social process of production—antagonistic not in the sense of individual antagonism, but of one arising from the social conditions of life of the individuals; at the same time the productive forces developing in the womb of bourgeois society create the material conditions for the solution of that antagonism.—P. E.

ANTAGONISM OF INTERESTS
We find that the hostile antagonism of interests is recognized as the basis of social organization.—M.

ANTIQUATED
The antiquated tries to maintain and re-establish itself within the new order.—Ltr. to Bolte.

ANTIQUITY
In antiquity, material productive labor bore the stigma of slavery and was regarded merely as a pedestal for the idle citizen.—C.4.

ANTI-SEMITISM
What is stated as theory in Jewish religion, namely, con-

tempt for theory, art, history and man as an end in himself, is an actual and conscious point of view, held to be virtuous by the man of money. Even the relations between the sexes, between man and woman, become an object of commerce. The law of the Jew, lacking all solid foundation, is only a religious caricature of morality and of law in general, but it provides the formal rites in which the world of property clothes its transactions.— J. Q.

APHORISTIC STYLE
The wealth and diversity of the subjects to be treated could have been compressed into *one* work only in a purely aphoristic style; whilst an aphoristic presentation of this kind, for its part, would have given the impression of arbitrary systematizing.—M.

APOSTASY
Every philosophy of the past without exception was accused by the theologians of apostasy.—L. A.

ASIATIC AGRICULTURE
In Asiatic empires we are quite accustomed to see agriculture deteriorating under one government and reviving again under some other government. There the harvests correspond to good or bad governments, as they change in Europe with good or bad seasons.—D. T.

The artificial fertilization of the Asiatic soil, dependent on a central government, and immediately decaying with the neglect of irrigation and drainage, explains the otherwise strange fact that we now find whole territories barren and desert that were once brilliantly cultivated, as Palmyra, Petra, the ruins in Yemen, and large provinces of Egypt,

Persia, and Hindustan; it also explains how a single war of devastation has been able to depopulate a country for centuries, and to strip it of all its civilization.—D. T.

ASIATIC ECONOMICS
An economical function developed upon all Asiatic governments: the function of providing public works.—D. T.

ASIATIC GOVERNMENT
There have been in Asia, generally, from immemorial times, but three departments of government: that of finance, or the plunder of the interior, that of war, or the plunder of the exterior; and, finally, the department of public works.—D. T.

ASIATIC SOCIAL REVOLUTION
England, it is true, in causing a social revolution in Hindustan, was actuated only by the vilest interests, and was stupid in her manner of enforcing them. But that is not the question. The question is, can mankind fulfill its destiny without a fundamental revolution in the social state of Asia? If not, whatever may have been the crimes of England she was the unconscious tool of history in bringing about that revolution.—D. T.

ASSOCIATION, AGRARIAN
Association, applied to land, shares the economic advantage of large-scale landed property, and first brings to realization the original tendency inherent in land division, namely, equality.—M.

AVARICE
The only wheels which political economy sets in motion are avarice and the war amongst the avaricious—competition.—M.

At the historical dawn of capitalist production—and every capitalist upstart has personally to go through this historical state—avarice, and the desire to get rich, are the ruling passions.—C. 1.

AVERAGE
The intelligible and the necessary wants to be recognized only as a blindly working *average*.—Ltr. to Kugelmann.

AVERAGE PROFIT
Experience shows that if a branch of industry, such as, say, the cotton industry, yields unusually high profits at one period, it makes very little profit, or even suffers losses, at another, so that in a certain cycle of years the average profit is much the same as in other branches. And capital soon learns to take this experience into account.—C. 3.

Average profit is the basic conception, the conception that capitals of equal magnitude must share *pro rata* to their magnitude in the total surplus-value squeezed out of the laborers by the total social capital; or that every individual capital should be regarded merely as a part of the total social capital, and every capitalist actually as a shareholder in the total social enterprise, each sharing in the total profit *pro rata* to the magnitude of his share of capital.—C. 3.

The average profit coincides with the average surplus-value produced for each 100 of capital. In the case of the average profit the value of the advanced capital becomes an additional element determining the rate of profit.—C. 3.

B

BACHELOR
He is an old bachelor through and through, anxiously concerned about his conservation and preservation.—Ltr. to Engels.

BACON
The real founder of English materialism and all modern experimental science was Bacon. For him natural science was true science and physics based on perception was the most excellent part of natural science.—H. F.

In Bacon, its first creator, materialism contained latent and still in a naive way the germs of all-around development. Matter smiled at man with poetical, sensuous brightness. The aphoristic doctrine itself, on the other hand, was full of the inconsistencies of theology.—H. F.

BAIT
Every product is a bait with which to seduce away the other's very being, his money; every real and possible need is a weakness which will lead the fly to the gluepot.—M.

BAKUNIN
On the whole Bakunin is one of the few fellows whom after sixteen years I find to have developed, not backwards, but further.—Ltr. to Engels.

Theory is for Bakunin only a secondary affair, merely a means to a self-asserting end. The less he is a scientist, the more he is an intriguer.—Ltr. to Bolte.

BARTER
The direct barter of products attains the elementary form of the relative expression of value in one respect, but not in another.— C. 1.

BEAUTY
Man also forms things in accordance with the laws of beauty—M.

BEGGARY
A section of the working class falls into the ranks of beggary just as necessarily as a section of the middle capitalists falls into the working class.—M.

BEING
The less you are, the more you have; the less you express your own life, the greater is your alienated life—the greater is the store of your estranged being.—M.

A being which does not have its nature outside itself is not a natural being, and plays no part in the system of nature. A being which has no object outside itself is not an objective being. A being which is not itself an object for some third being has no being for its object; i. e., it is not objectively related. Its being is not objective.—M.

An unobjective being is a nullity—an un-being. Suppose a being which is neither an object itself, nor has an object. Such a being, in the first place, would be the unique being: there would exist no being outside it—it would exist solitary and alone. For as soon as there are objects outside me, as soon as I am not alone, I am another—another reality than the object outside me. For this third object I am thus another reality than it; that is, I am its object. Thus, to suppose a being which is not the object of another being is to presuppose that no objective being exists.—M.

BELLUM OMNIUM

In the animal kingdom, the bellum omnium contra omnes more or less preserves the conditions of existence of every species.—C. 1.

BOOKKEEPING

Apart from the actual buying and selling, labor-time is expended in bookkeeping, which besides absorbs materialized labor such as pens, ink, paper, desks, office paraphernalia.—C. 2.

Bookkeeping includes the determination of prices, or the calculation of the prices of commodities.—C. 2.

Bookkeeping, as the control and ideal synthesis of the process of production, becomes the more necessary the more the process assumes a social scale and loses its purely individual character. It is therefore more necessary in capitalist production than in the scattered production of handicraft and peasant economy, more necessary in collective (communist) production than in capitalist production.—C. 2.

BOURGEOIS ACCOMPLISHMENT

The bourgeoisie has been the first to show what man's activity can bring about. It has accomplished *wonders* far surpassing Egyptian pyramids, Roman aqueducts, and Gothic cathedrals; it has conducted expeditions that put in the shade all former Exoduses of nations and crusades.—C. M.

BOURGEOIS ARGUMENTS

"Undoubtedly," it will be said, "religious, moral, philosophical and juridical ideas have been modified in the course of historical development. But religion, morality, philosophy, political science, and law constantly survived this change. There are, besides, eternal truths, such as Freedom, Justice, etc., that are common to all states of society. But communism abolishes eternal truths, it abolishes all religion, all morality, instead of constituting them on a new basis; it therefore acts in contradiction to all past historical experience."—C. M.

BOURGEOIS CHEAPNESS

The cheap prices of its commodities are the heavy artillery with which it batters down all Chinese walls, with which it forces the barbarians' intensely obstinate hatred of foreigners to capitulate.—C. M.

BOURGEOIS CONVERSION

The bourgeoisie has stripped of its halo every occupation hitherto honored and looked up to with reverent awe. It has converted the physician, the lawyer, the priest, the poet, the man of science, into its paid wage-laborers.—C. M.

BOURGEOIS DUPLICITY

The relations of productions in which the bourgeoisie exists have not a single, a simple character, but a double character, a character of duplicity; in the same relations in which wealth is produced, poverty is produced also; in the same relations in which there is a development of productive forces, there is a productive force of repression; these relations produce bourgeois wealth, that is to say the wealth of the bourgeois class, only in continually annihilating the wealth of integral members of that class and in producing an ever-growing proletariat.—P. P.

BOURGEOIS INSTITUTIONS
State, church, etc., are only justified insofar as they are committees to superintend or administer the common interests of the productive bourgeoisie; and their costs— since by their nature these costs belong to the overhead costs of production—must be reduced to the unavoidable minimum.—C. 4.

BOURGEOIS INTERNATIONALISM
Just as the bourgeoisie has made the country dependent on the towns, so it has made barbarian and semi-barbarian countries dependent on the civilized ones, nations of peasants on nations of bourgeois, the East on the West.—C. M.

BOURGEOIS MISCONCEPTION
Selfish misconception induces you to transform into eternal laws of nature and of reason the social forms springing from your present mode of production and form of property.—C. M.

BOURGEOIS SELF-CONTRADICTION
Modern bourgeois society is like the sorcerer, who is no longer able to control the power of the nether world whom he has called up by his spells. For many a decade past the

history of industry and commerce is but the history of the revolt of modern productive forces against modern conditions of production, against the (private) property relations.—C. M.

C

CAPITAL
Capital is not a personal, it is a social power.—C. M.

Capital is stored-up labor.—M.

The essential condition for the existence, and for the sway, of the bourgeois class is the formation and augmentation of capital. —C. M.

Capital is the governing power over labor and its products. The capitalist possesses the power, not on account of his personal or human qualities, but inasmuch as he is an owner of capital. His power is the purchasing power of his capital, which nothing can withstand.—M.

People who do not own capital, tackle it quite differently than the owner, who anxiously weighs the limitations of his private capital in so far as he handles it himself.—C. 3.

As a matter of history, capital, as opposed to landed property, invariably takes the form at first of money; it appears as moneyed wealth, as the capital of the merchant and of the usurer. But we have no need to refer to the origin of capital in order to discover that the first form of appearance of capital is money.—C. 1.

CAPITAL, SIZE OF
The larger size of his capital compensates the biggest capitalist for the smaller profits.—M.

CAPITAL, SOCIAL CHARACTER OF
Capital announces from its first appearance a new epoch in the process of social production.—C. 1.

To be a capitalist is to have not only a purely personal, but a social status in production. Capital is a collective product, and only by the united action of many members, nay, in the last resort, only by the united action of all members of society, can it be set in motion.—C. M.

The social character of capital is first promoted and wholly realized through the full development of the credit and banking system.—C. 3.

By means of the banking system the distribution of capital as a special business, a social function, is taken out of the hands of the private capitalists.—C. 3.

CAPITAL AND PRODUCTION
With the accumulation of capital, the specifically capitalistic mode of production develops, and with the capitalistic mode of production the accumulation of capital.—C. 1.

On the one hand it is the tendency of capital to reduce to a dwindling minimum the labor-time necessary for the production of commodities, and therefore also the number of the productive population in relation to the amount of the product. On the other hand, however, the capitalist mode of production has the opposite tendency to accumulate, to transform profit into capital, to appropriate the greatest possible quantity of the labor of others. It strives to reduce the norm of necessary labor, but to employ the greatest possible quantity of productive labor at a given norm.—C.4.

We have seen not only how capital produces, but how it itself is produced, and how, as an essentially altered relation, it emerges from the process of production and how it is developed in it. On the one hand capital transforms the mode of production; on the other hand this changed form of the mode of production and a particular stage in the development of the material forces of production are the basis and precondition, the premise, for its own formation.—C. 4.

CLASS WAR
In depicting the most general phases of the development of the proletariat, we traced the more or less veiled civil war, ranging within existing society, up to the point where that war breaks out into open revolution, and where the violent overthrow of the bourgeoisie lays the foundation for the sway of the proletariat.—C. M.

CLASSES
The existence of classes is connected with particular, historic phases in the development of production.—Ltr. to Weydmeyer.

The first question to be answered is this: What constitutes a class—and the reply to this follows naturally from the reply to another question, namely: What makes wage-laborers, capitalists and landlords constitute the three great social classes? At first glance—the identity of revenues and sources of revenue. There are three great social groups whose members, the individuals forming them, live on wages, profit and ground-rent respectively, on the realization of their labor-power, their capital, and their landed property. However, from this standpoint, physicians and officials, e.g., would also constitute two classes, for they belong to two distinct social groups, the members of each of these groups receiving their revenue from one and the same source.—C. 3.

CLASSICAL ECONOMY
Accumulation for accumulation's sake, production for production's sake: by this formula classical economy expressed the historical mission of the bourgeoisie.—C. 1.

CLASSLESS SOCIETY
In a future society, the antagonisms of classes will have ceased, there will no longer be classes.—P. P.

If the proletariat during its contest with the bourgeoisie is compelled, by the force of circumstances, to organize itself as a class, if, by means of revolution, it makes itself a ruling class, and, as such, sweeps away by force the old conditions of production, then it will, along with these conditions, have swept away the conditions for the existence of class antagonism, and of classes generally, and will thereby have abolished its own supremacy as a class.—C. M.

CLIMATE
The more unfavorable the climate, the more congested is the working period in agriculture, and hence the shorter is the time in which capital and labor are expended. Take

Russia for instance. In some of the northern districts of that country field labor is possible only from 130 to 150 days throughout the year, and it may be imagined what a loss Russia would sustain if 50 out of the 65 millions of her European population remained without work during the six or eight months of the winter, when agricultural labor is at a standstill.—C. 2.

CLOCK
The clock is the first automatic machine applied to practical purposes.—Ltr. to Engels.

CLOTHING
Wherever the want of clothing forced them to it, the human race made clothes for thousands of years, without a single man becoming a tailor. But coats and linen, like every other element of material wealth that is the spontaneous produce of nature, must invariably owe their existence to a special productive activity, exercised with a definite aim, an activity that appropriates particular nature-given materials to particular human wants.—C. 1.

Whether the coat be worn by the tailor or by his customer, in either case it operates as a use-value.—C. 1.

COAL
When a coal mine supplies coal to an ironworks and gets from the latter iron which enters into the operations of the coal mine as means of production, the coal is in this way exchanged for capital to the amount of its own value, is exchanged as capital for coal.—C.4.

COIN
That money takes the shape of coin springs from its function as the circulation medium.—C. 1.

COMMODITY, VALUE OF
The value of a commodity represents human labor in the abstract, the expenditure of human labor in general.—C. 1.

The value of each commodity is determined by the quantity of labor expended on and materialized in it, by the working-time necessary, under given social conditions, for its production.—C. 1.

Commodities, in which equal quantities of labor are embodied, or which can be produced in the same time, have the same value. The value of one commodity is to the value of any other, as the labor-time necessary for the production of the one is to that necessary for the production of the other.—C. 1.

COMMODITY MAN
Production does not simply produce man as a commodity, the commodity man, man in the role of a commodity; it produces him in keeping with this role as a spiritually and physically dehumanized being.—M.

COMMON INTEREST
The common interest is appreciated by each only so long as he gains more by it than without it. And unity of action ceases the moment one or the other side becomes the weaker, when each tries to extricate himself on his own as advantageously as he possibly can. Again, if one produces more cheaply and can sell more goods, thus possessing

himself of a greater place in the market by selling below the current market-price, he will do so, and will thereby begin a movement which gradually compels the others to introduce the cheaper mode of production, and one which reduces the socially necessary labor to a new, and lower, level. If one side has the advantage, all belonging to it gain. It is as though they exerted their common monopoly.—C. 3.

COMMON OWNERSHIP
Haxthausen discovered common ownership of land in Russia, Maurer proved it to be the social foundation from which all Teutonic races started in history.—C. M.

COMMUNE
"Commune" was the name taken in France by the nascent towns even before they had conquered from their feudal lords and masters local self-government and political rights as the "Third Estate."—C. M.

The working class did not expect miracles from the *Commune.* They have no ready-made utopias to introduce by decree of the people. They have *no ideals* to realize, but to set free the elements of the new society with which old collapsing bourgeois society is pregnant.—C. W.

COMMUNISM
Communism is the positive expression of annulled private property.—M.

Communism differs from all previous movements in that it overturns the basis of all earlier relations of production, and for the first time consciously treats all natural premises as the creatures of man and strips them of their natural character and subjugates them to the power of individuals united.

Its organization is, therefore, essentially economic, the material production of the conditions of this unity.—C. 1.

The communists never cease, for a single moment, to instill into the working class the clearest possible recognition of the hostile antagonism between bourgeoisie and proletariat.—C. M.

The communists everywhere support every revolutionary movement against the existing social and political order of things.—C. M.

Communism begins from the outset with atheism; but atheism is at first far from being communism; indeed, it is still mostly an abstraction.—M.

Communism as the positive transcendence of private property, as human self-estrangement, and therefore as the real appropriation of human essence by and for man; communism therefore is the complete return of man to himself as a social (i.e., human) being—a return become conscious, and accomplished within the entire wealth of previous development.—M.

Communism is the riddle of history solved, and it knows itself to be this solution.—M.

In order to abolish the idea of private property, the idea of communism is completely sufficient. It takes actual communist action to abolish actual private property. History will come to it; and this movement, which in theory we already know to be a self-transcending movement, will constitute in actual fact a very severe and protracted process. But we must regard it as a real advance to have gained beforehand a consciousness of the limited character as well as of the goal of this historical movement—and a consciousness which reaches out beyond it.—M.

Communism is . . . the negation of the negation, and is hence the actual phase necessary for the next stage of historical development in the process of human emancipation and recovery. Communism is the necessary pattern and the dynamic principle of the *immediate* future, but communism as such is *not* the goal of human development—the structure of human society.—M.

This communism, as fully developed naturalism, equals humanism, and as fully developed humanism equals naturalism; it is the genuine resolution of the conflict between man and nature and between man and man—the true resolution of the strife between existence and essence, between objectification and self-confirmation, between freedom and necessity, between the individual and the species.—M.

COMMUNISM, ACCUSATION OF
Where is the party in opposition that has not been decried as communistic by its opponents in power? Where the opposition that has not hurled back the branding reproach of communism, against the more advanced opposition parties, as well as against its reactionary adversaries?—C. M.

COMMUNISM, CRUDE
The first positive annulment of private property-crude communism—is merely one form in which the vileness of private property, which wants to set itself up as the positive community, comes to the surface.—M.

COMMUNISM, IMMATURE

The other, still immature communism, meanwhile seeks an historical proof for itself—a proof in the realm of the existent—amongst disconnected historical phenomena opposed to private property, tearing single phases from the historical process and focusing attention on them as proofs of its historical pedigree. By so doing it simply makes clear that by far the greater part of this process contradicts its claims, and that, if it has once been, precisely its being in the past refutes its pretension to being essential.—M.

COMMUNIST AIM

The immediate aim of the communists is the same as that of all the other proletarian parties: formation of the proletariat into a class, overthrow of the bourgeois supremacy, conquest of political power by the proletariat.—C. M.

COMMUNIST CONCLUSIONS

The theoretical conclusions of the communists are in no way based on ideas or principles that have been invented, or discovered, by this or that would-be universal reformer. They merely express, in general terms, actual relations springing from an existing class struggle, from a historical movement going on under our very eyes.—C. M.

COMMUNIST MANIFESTO

It is high time that communists should openly, in the face of the whole world, publish their views, their aims, their tendencies, and meet the nursery tale of the Specter of Communism with a Manifesto of the party itself.—C. M.

COMMUNIST MOTTO

Working men of all countries, unite!—C. M.

COMMUNIST POWER
Communism is already acknowledged by all European Powers to be itself a Power.—C. M.

COMMUNIST PROGRAM
The theory of the Communists may be summed up in the single sentence: abolition of private property.—C. M.

Theoretically, the communists have over the great mass of the proletariat the advantage of clearly understanding the line of march, the conditions, and the ultimate general results of the proletarian movement.—C. M.

COMMUNIST REVOLUTION
The communists disdain to conceal their views and aims. They openly declare that their ends can be attained only by the forcible overthrow of all existing social conditions. Let the ruling classes tremble at a communist revolution. The proletarians have nothing to lose but their chains. They have a world to win—C. M.

COMMUNIST SPECTER
A specter is haunting Europe—the specter of communism. All the powers of old Europe have entered into a holy alliance to exorcise this specter.—C. M.

COMMUNIST WORKMEN
When communist workmen associate with one another, theory, propaganda, etc., is their first end. But at the same time, as a result of this association, they acquire a new need—the need for society—and what appears as a means becomes an end.—M.

COMMUNISTS

The communists do not form a separate party opposed to other working-class parties. They have no interest separate and apart from those of the proletariat as a whole. They do not set up any sectarian principles of their own, by which to shape and mold the proletarian movement.—C. M.

COMPENSATION

Concerning the relationship between worker and capitalist one should add that the capitalist is more than compensated for the raising of wages by the reduction in the amount of labor-time. —M.

The more hazardous lines pay higher insurance rates, and recover them in the prices of their commodities. In practice all this means that every circumstance, which renders one line of production—and all of them are considered equally necessary within certain limits—less profitable, and another more profitable, is taken into account once and for all as valid ground for compensation, without always requiring the renewed action of competition to justify the motives or factors for calculating this compensation.—C. 3.

COMPETITION

Competition is only possible if capitals are held in many hands. —M.

Competition is not industrial emulation, it is commercial emulation.—P. P.

Competition compels the producer to sell the product of two hours as cheaply as the product of one hour.—P. P.

Competition always tends to level the rate of profits, which can rise only temporarily above the ordinary rate.—P. P.

Since we already know that monopoly prices are as high as possible, since the interest of the capitalists, even from the point of view commonly held by political economists, stands in hostile opposition to society, and since a rise of profit operates like compound interest on the price of the commodity, it follows that the sole defense against the capitalists is competition, which according to the evidence of political economy acts beneficently by both raising wages and lowering the prices of commodities to the advantage of the consuming public.—M.

Competition can influence the rate of profit only to the extent that it affects the prices of commodities. Competition can only make the producers within the same sphere of production sell their commodities at the same prices, and make them sell their commodities in different spheres of production at prices which will give them the same profit, the same proportional addition to the price of commodities which has already been partially determined by wages. Hence competition can only equalize inequalities in the rate of profit.—C. 3.

Competition, according to an American economist, determines how many days of simple labor are contained in a day of complex labor.—P. P.

Competition lowers the prices of commodities to the advantage of the consuming public.—M.

The sole defense against the capitalists is *competition*.—M.

The side of competition which happens for the moment to be weaker is also the side in which the individual acts independently of, and often directly against, the mass of his competitors, and precisely in this manner is the dependence of one upon the other impressed upon them, while the stronger side acts always more or less as a united whole against its antagonist. If the demand for this particular kind of commodity is greater than the supply, one buyer outbids another—within certain limits—and so raises the price of the commodity for all of them above the market-value, while on the other hand the sellers unite in trying to sell at a high market-price. If, conversely, the supply exceeds the demand, one begins to dispose of his goods at a cheaper rate and the others must follow, while the buyers unite in their efforts to depress the market-price as much as possible below the market-value.—C. 3.

The battle of competition is fought by cheapening of commodities. The cheapness of commodities depends, *ceteris paribus*, on the productiveness of labor, and this again on the scale of production. Therefore, the larger capitals beat the smaller. . . . It always ends in the ruin of many small capitalists, whose capitals partly pass into the hand of their conquerors, partly vanish.—C. 1.

Competition engenders poverty, foments civil war; it disturbs families, corrupts the public conscience, "changes the natural zones," confounds nationalities, "overturns the notions of equity, of justice," of morality, and what is worse, it destroys honest and free commerce and does not even give in exchange synthetical value, fixed and honest price. It disenchants everybody, even the economists. It forces things on, even to its own destruction.—P. P.

The consumer is not more free than the producer. His choice depends upon his means and his wants. The one and the other are determined by his social position, which itself depends upon the entire social organization.—P. P.

CONSUMER NECESSITY

For our purposes we may call this entire subdivision consumer necessities, regardless of whether such a product as tobacco is really a consumer necessity from the physiological point of view. It suffices that it is habitually such.—C. 2.

CONSUMPTION

There would be no production without consumption.—M.

The capitalist produces with absolutely no direct regard for consumption.—C. 4.

From a social point of view the working class is just as much an appendage of capital as the ordinary instruments of labor. Even its individual consumption is a mere factor in the process of production. That process, however, takes good care to prevent these self-conscious instruments from leaving it in the lurch, for it removes their product, as fast as it is made, from their pole to the opposite pole of capital. Individual consumption provides, on the one hand, the means for their maintenance and reproduction: on the other hand, it secures by the annihilation of the necessaries of life, the continued reappearance of the workman in the labor-market.—C. 1.

The individual consumption of the laborer, whether it proceed within the workshop or outside it, whether it be part of the process of production or not, forms a factor of the production and reproduction of capital; just cleaning machinery does, whether it be done while the machinery is working or while it is standing. The fact that the laborer consumes his means of subsistence for his own purposes, and not to please the capitalist, has no bearing on the matter. The consumption of food by a beast of burden is none the less a necessary factor in the process of production, because the beast enjoys what it eats.—C. 1.

The capitalist considers that part alone of the laborer's individual consumption to be productive which is requisite for the perpetuation of the class, and which therefore must take place in order that the capitalist may have labor power to consume; what the laborer consumes for his own pleasure beyond that part is unproductive consumption. If the accumulation of capital were to cause a rise of wages and an increase in the laborer's consumption, unaccompanied by increase in the consumption of labor power by capital, an additional capital would be consumed unproductively.—C. 1.

Productive consumption is distinguished from individual consumption by this, that the latter uses up products, as means of subsistence for the living individual; the former, as means whereby alone labor, the labor power of the living individual, is enabled to act. The product, therefore, of individual consumption, is the consumer himself; the result of productive consumption is a product distinct from the consumer.—C. 1.

CONSUMPTION, PRIVATE
So far as the capitalist's actions are a mere function of capital—endowed as capital is, in his person, with consciousness and a will—his own private consumption is a robbery perpetrated on accumulation, just as in bookkeeping by double entry, the private expenditure of the capitalist is

placed on the debtor side of his account against his capital. To accumulate is to conquer the world of social wealth, to increase the mass of human beings exploited by him, and thus to extend both the direct and the indirect sway of the capitalist.—C. 1.

CONSUMPTION AND WEALTH
Real political economy à la Smith treats the capitalist only as personified capital. But who is to consume the products? The laborers?—but they don't. The capitalist himself? Then he is acting as a big idle consumer and not as a capitalist. The owners of land and money rents? They do not reproduce their consumption, and thereby are of disservice to wealth. Nevertheless, there are also two correct aspects in this contradictory view, which regards the capitalist only as a real amasser of wealth, not an illusory one like the miser proper: (1) capital is treated only as an agent for the development of the productive forces and of production; (2) it expresses the standpoint of emerging capitalist society, to which what matters is exchange-value, not use-value; wealth, not enjoyment. The enjoyment of wealth seems to be a superfluous luxury, until it itself learns to combine exploitation and consumption and to subordinate itself to the enjoyment of wealth.—C. 4.

CONTRADICTION, CAPITALIST
The contradiction of the capitalist mode of production lies precisely in its tendency toward an absolute development of the productive forces, which continually come into conflict with the specific conditions of production in which capital moves, and alone can move.—C. 3.

CONTRIVED APPETITES
The extension of products and needs falls into contriving refined, unnatural and imaginary appetites.—M.

CONTROL, CAPITALIST
The control exercised by the capitalist is not only a special function, due to the nature of the social labor-process, and peculiar to that process, but it is, at the same time, a function of the exploitation of a social labor-process, and is consequently rooted in the unavoidable antagonism between the exploiter and the living and laboring raw material he exploits.—C. 1.

CONTROVERSY, ECONOMIC
Of course a controversy now arises in the field of political economy. The one side recommends luxury and execrates thrift. The other recommends thrift and execrates luxury. But the former admits that it wants luxury in order to produce labor (i.e., absolute thrift); and the latter admits that it recommends thrift in order to produce wealth (i.e., luxury).—M.

CONVERSION OF NATURE
Advancing human labor converts the product of nature into the manufactured product of nature.—M.

CREATION
The Creation is an idea very difficult to dislodge from popular consciousness. The self-mediated being of nature and of man is incomprehensible to it, because it contradicts everything palpable in practical life.—M.

CREDIT
The credit which a big capitalist enjoys compared with a smaller one means for him all the greater saving in fixed

capital—that is, in the amount of ready money he must always have at hand.—M.

CREDIT SYSTEM

With capitalist production an altogether new force comes into play—the credit system. In its beginnings, the credit system sneaks in as a modest helper of accumulation and draws by invisible threads the money resources scattered all over the surface of society into the hands of individual or associated capitalists. But soon it becomes a new and formidable weapon in the competitive struggle, and finally it transforms itself into an immense social mechanism for the centralization of capitals.—C. 1.

Simultaneously with the development of capitalist production the credit system also develops. The money-capital which the capitalist cannot as yet employ in his own business is employed by others, who pay him interest for its use. It serves him as money-capital in its specific meaning, as a kind of capital distinguished from productive capital. But it serves as capital in another's hand.—C. 2.

The credit system appears as the main lever of overproduction and overspeculation in commerce solely because the reproduction process, which is elastic by nature, is here forced to its extreme limits, and is so forced because a large part of the social capital is employed by people who do not own it and who consequently tackle things quite differently than the owner, who anxiously weighs the limitations of his private capital in so far as he handles it himself.—C. 3.

D

DARWIN
Darwin's book is of utmost importance and provides me with a foundation in natural science for the class struggles in history.—Ltr. to Lassalle.

Darwin has interested us in the history of nature's technology, i.e., in the formation of the organs of plants and animals, which organs serve as instruments of production for sustaining life.—C. 1.

DEATH
Death seems to be a harsh victory of the species over the definite individual and to contradict their unity. But the determinate individual is only a determinate species being, and as such mortal.—M.

DECENTRALIZING EFFECT
The process of accumulation and concentration of capital would soon bring about the collapse of capitalist production if it were not for counteracting tendencies, which have a continuous decentralizing effect alongside the centripetal one.—C. 3.

DECLINE OF PROFIT

The drop in the rate of profit is not due to an absolute, but only to a relative decrease of the variable part of the total capital, i.e., to its decrease in relation to the constant part.—C. 3.

DESPOTISM, BOURGEOIS

Masses of laborers, crowded into the factory, are organized like soldiers. As privates of the industrial army they are placed under the command of a perfect hierarchy of officers and sergeants. Not only are they the slaves of the bourgeois class, and of the bourgeois state, they are daily and hourly enslaved by the machine, by the overlooker, and, above all, by the individual bourgeois manufacturer himself. The more openly this despotism proclaims gain to be its end and aim, the more petty, the more hateful and the more embittered it is.—C. M.

DESTITUTION, PROLETARIAN

In the gravitation of market-price to natural price it is the worker who loses most of all and necessarily. And it is just the capacity of the capitalist to direct his capital into another channel which renders destitute the worker who is restricted to some particular branch of labor, or forces him to submit to every demand of this capitalist. The accidental and sudden fluctuations in market-price hit rent less than they do that part of the price which is resolved into profit and wages; but they hit profit less than they do wages. In most cases, for every wage that rises, one remains stationary and one falls.—M.

Even in the condition of society most favorable to the worker, the inevitable result for the worker is overwork and premature death, decline to a mere machine, a bond servant of capital, which piles up dangerously over against him, more competition, and for a section of the workers starvation or beggary.—M.

DESTRUCTION OF CAPITAL

Overproduction of capital is never anything more than overproduction—of means of labor and necessities of life—which may serve as capital, i.e., may serve to exploit labor at a given degree of exploitation; a fall in the intensity of exploitation below a certain point, however, calls forth disturbances, crises, and destruction of capital.—C. 3.

DISPLACEMENT OF WORKMEN

So soon as machinery sets free a part of the workmen employed in a given branch of industry, the reserve men are also diverted into new channels of employment, and become absorbed in other branches; meanwhile the original victims, during the period of transition, for the most part starve and perish.—C. 1.

Machinery displaces labor and increases the net revenue; it reduces the number of laborers and increases the products. So this would be desirable. But no. In that case it must be shown that machinery does not deprive the laborers of bread. And how is this to be shown? By the fact that after a shock (to which perhaps the section of the population which is directly affected cannot offer any resistance) machinery once again employs more people than were employed before it was introduced—and therefore once again increases the number of "productive laborers" and restores the former disproportion. That is in fact what happens.—C. 4.

A whole series of bourgeois economists insists that all machinery that displaces workmen simultaneously and necessarily sets free an amount of capital adequate to employ the same identical workmen. The real facts, which are travestied by the optimism of economists, are as follows: The laborers, when driven out of the workshop by the machinery, are thrown upon the labor market, and there add to the number of workmen at the disposal of the capitalists. . . . Even should they find employment, what a poor look-out is theirs! Crippled as they are by division of labor, these poor devils are worth so little outside their old trade, that they cannot find admission into any industries, except a few of inferior kind, that are oversupplied with underpaid workmen.—C. 1.

Although machinery necessarily throws men out of work in those industries into which it is introduced, yet it may, notwithstanding this, bring about an increase of employment in other industries. This effect, however, has nothing in common with the so-called theory of compensation.—C. 1.

As the use of machinery extends in a given industry, the immediate effect is to increase production in the other industries that furnish the first with means of production. How far employment is thereby found for an increased number of men, depends, given the length of the working day and the intensity of labor, on the composition of the capital employed.—C. 1.

DISRAELI

For some time, Mr. Disraeli affects an awful solemnity of speech, an elaborate slowness of utterance and a passionless method of formality, which, however consistent they may be with his peculiar notions of the dignity becoming a Minister in expectance, are really distressing to his tortured audience. Once he succeeded in giving even commonplaces the pointed appearance of epigrams. Now he contrives to bury even epigrams in the conventional dullness of respectability. An orator who, like Mr. Disraeli, excels in handling the danger rather than in wielding the sword, should have been the last to forget Voltaire's warning, that "All styles are good save the tiresome kind."—D. T.

DISSOLUTION, INDUSTRIAL
At a certain stage of development, the petty mode of production brings forth the material agencies for its own dissolution. From that moment new forces and new passions spring up in the bosom of society; but the old social organization fetters them and keeps them down. It must be annihilated; it is annihilated.—C. 1.

DISTRIBUTION
The mode of the distribution of the social product will vary the productive organization of the community, and the degree of historical development attained by the producers.—C. 1.

DISTURBANCES, SOCIAL
In capitalist society where social reason always asserts itself only *post festum*, great disturbances may and must constantly occur.—C. 2.

E

EARNINGS
Whilst the rent of the lazy landowner usually amounts to a third of the product of the soil, and the profit of the busy capitalist to as much as twice the interest on money, the "something more" which the worker himself earns at the best of times amounts to so little that of four children of his, two must starve and die. Whilst according to the political economists it is solely through labor that man enhances the value of the products of nature, whilst labor is man's active property, according to this same political economy the landowner and the capitalist, who *qua* landowner and capitalist are merely privileged and idle gods, are everywhere superior to the worker and lay down the law to him.—M.

EASY MONEY MARKET
An easy money market calls enterprises into being en masse.—C. 2.

ECONOMIC FORMS
Natural economy, money-economy, the credit-economy have been placed in opposition to one another as being the

three characteristic economic forms of movement in social production.—C. 2.

ECONOMIC STRUCTURE

The economic structure of capitalistic society has grown out of the economic structure of feudal society. The dissolution of the latter set free the elements of the former.—C. 1.

ECONOMICS

The material of the economists is the active and busy life of men.—P. P.

ECONOMISTS, FATALIST

We have the fatalist economists, who in their theory are as indifferent to what they call the inconveniences of bourgeois production as the bourgeois themselves are, in actual practice, to the sufferings of the proletarians who assist them to acquire riches.—P. P.

ECONOMIST'S CONTRADICTION

The political economist tells us that originally and in theory the whole produce of labor belongs to the worker. But at the same time he tells us that in actual fact what the worker gets is the smallest and utterly indispensable part of the product—as much, only, as is necessary for his existence, not as a man but as a worker, and for the propagation, not of humanity, but of the slave-class of workers.—M.

Whilst according to the political economists it is solely through labor that man enhances the value of the products of nature, according to this same political economy the landowner and the capitalist are everywhere superior to the worker.—M.

The political economist tells us that everything is bought with labor and that capital is nothing but accumulated labor; but at the same time he tells us that the worker, far from being able to buy everything, must sell himself and his human identity.—M.

ECONOMY

The capitalist's fantatical insistence on economy in means of production is quite understandable. That nothing is lost or wasted and the means of production are consumed only in the manner required by production itself depends partly on the skill and intelligence of the laborers and partly on the discipline enforced by the capitalist for the combined labor. This discipline will become superfluous under a social system in which the laborers work for their own account.—C. 3.

EDUCATION, COMMUNIST

And your education! Is not that also social, and determined by the social conditions under which you educate, by the intervention, direct or indirect, of society by means of schools, etc.? The communists have not invented the intervention of society in education; they do but seek to alter the character of that intervention, and to rescue education from the influence of the ruling class.—C. M.

EDUCATION, COST OF

If I buy the service of a teacher not to develop my faculties but to acquire some skill with which I can earn money—or if others buy this teacher for me—and if I really learn something (which in itself is quite independent of the payment for the service), then these costs of education, just as the costs of my maintenance, belong to the costs of production of my labor power.—C. 4.

EDUCATOR
The educator himself needs educating.—T. F.

EGOTISTICAL MAN
The recognition of the freedom of egotistical man is the recognition of the unrestrained movement of spiritual and material elements that form its content.—J. Q.

ELASTICITY, ECONOMIC
Finally, all the springs of (capitalist) production act with greater elasticity, the more its scale extends with the mass of the capital advanced.—C. 1.

EMANCIPATION
Political emancipation is a great goal. It is not the ultimate form of human emancipation, but it is the ultimate form within the present world order. And let it be understood that we mean real, practical emancipation.—J. Q.

Human emancipation is achieved only when the individual gives up being an abstract citizen and becomes a member of his species as individual man in his daily life and work and situation, when he recognizes and organizes his *"forces propres,"* his own strength, as part of the forces of society, which are then no longer separated from him as a political power.—J. Q.

EMANCIPATION, GERMAN
As philosophy finds its material weapon in the proletariat, so the proletariat finds its spiritual weapon in philosophy. And once the lightning of thought has squarely struck this ingenious soil of the people, the emancipation of the Germans into men will be accomplished.—C. C.

EMOTION

The dominion of the objective being in me, the sensuous outburst of my essential activity, is emotion, which thus becomes here the activity of my being.—M.

EMPIRICAL WORLD

If man draws all his knowledge, sensation, etc., from the world of the senses and the experience gained in it, the empirical world must be arranged so that in it man experiences and gets used to what is really human and that he becomes aware of himself as man.—H. F.

EMPIRICISM

Empiric observation must in every single case reveal the connection of the social and political organization with production, empirically and without any mystification of speculation.—G. I.

It is hardly necessary to assure the reader conversant with political economy that my results have been won by means of a wholly empirical analysis based on a conscientious critical study of the political economy.—M.

EMPLOYMENT

As the use of machinery extends in a given industry, the immediate effect is to increase production in the other industries that furnish the first with means of production. How far employment is thereby found for an increased number of men depends on the composition of the capital employed.—C. 1.

EXCRETIONS OF PRODUCTION

The capitalist mode of production extends the utilization of the excretions of production and consumption. By the former we mean the waste of industry and agriculture, and by the latter partly the excretions produced by the natural exchange of matter in the human body and partly the form of objects that remains after their consumption. In the chemical industry, for instance, excretions of production are such by-products as are wasted in production on a smaller scale; iron filings accumulating in the manufacture of machinery and returning into the production of iron as raw material, etc.—C. 3.

The economy of the excretions of production is to be distinguished from economy through the prevention of waste, that is to say, the reduction of excretions of production to a minimum, and the immediate utilization to a maximum of all raw and auxiliary materials required in production.—C. 3.

EXPLOITATION
General *exploitation* of communal human nature, like every imperfection in man, is a bond with heaven—an avenue giving the priest access to his heart.—M.

Every enterprise engaged in commodity production becomes at the same time an enterprise exploiting labor power. But only the capitalist production of commodities has become an epoch-making mode of *exploitation*, which, in the course of its historical development, revolutionizes, through the organization of the labor-process and the enormous improvement of technique, the entire economic structure of society in a manner eclipsing all former epochs.—C. 2.

Once discovered, the law of the deviation of the magnetic needle in the field of an electric current, or the law of magnetization of iron, around which an electric current circulates, cost never a penny. But the *exploitation* of these laws for the purposes of telegraphy, etc., necessitates a costly and expensive apparatus.—C. 1.

EXPLOITATION, BOURGEOIS

No sooner is the exploitation of the laborer by the manufacturer so far at an end, that he receives his wages in cash, than he is set upon by the other portions of the bourgeoisie, the landlord the shopkeeper, the pawnbroker, etc.—C. M.

For exploitation, veiled by religious and political illusions, the bourgeoisie has substituted naked, shameless, direct, brutal exploitation.—C. M.

EXPLOITATION OF LABOR

The degree of exploitation of labor, the appropriation of surplus-value and surplus-labor, is raised notably by lengthening the working day and intensifiying labor.—C. 3.

The rate of surplus-value is an exact expression for the degree of exploitation of labor power by capital, or of the laborer by the capitalist.—C. 1.

EXPROPRIATION OF THE MASSES

The annihilation of the old social organization, the transformation of the individualized and scattered means of production into socially concentrated ones, of the pygmy property of the many into the huge property of the few, the expropriation of the great mass of the people from the soil, from the means of subsistence, and from the means of labor, this fearful and painful expropriation of the mass of the people forms the prelude to the history of capital.—C. 1.

EXTRACTIVE INDUSTRY
That industry in which the material for labor is provided directly by nature, such as mining, hunting, fishing, and agriculture (so far as the latter is confined to breaking up virgin soil).—C. 1.

F

FACTORY DISCIPLINE
The barrack discipline is elaborated into a complete system in the factory.—C. 1.

FACTORY SYSTEM
The factory system is the essence of industry—of labor—brought to its maturity.—M.

The revolution in the instruments of labor attains its most highly developed form in the organized system of machinery in a factory.—C. 1.

Modern industry has converted the little workshop of the patriarchal master into the great factory of the industrial capitalist.— C. M.

In the factory tools make use of the workman.—C. 1.

The increase in the class of people wholly dependent on work intensifies competition among them, thus lowering their price. In the factory system this situation of the worker reaches its climax.—M.

FACTORY WORK
At the same time that factory work exhausts the nervous system to the uttermost, it does away with the many-sided play of the muscles, and confiscates every atom of freedom, both in bodily and intellectual activity. . . . Every kind of capitalist production insofar as it is not only a labor-process, but also a process of creating surplus-value, has this in common, that it is not the workman that employs the instruments of labor, but the instruments of labor that employ the workman.—C. 1.

FACTORY WORKER
The special skill of each individual insignificant factory operative vanishes as an infinitesimal quantity before the science, the gigantic physical forces, and the mass of labor that are embodied in the factory mechanism and, together with that mechanism, constitute the power of the "master."—C. 1.

FAITH
It is faith that brings salvation.—C. 3.

FALLING PROFIT
The capitalist mode of production produces a progressive decrease of the variable capital as compared to the constant capital, and consequently a continuously rising organic composition of the total capital. The immediate result of this is that the rate of surplus-value, at the same time, or even a rising degree of labor exploitation, is represented by a continually falling general rate of profit. The progressive tendency of the general rate of profit to fall is, therefore, just

an expression peculiar to the capitalist mode of production of the progressive development of the social productivity of labor.—C. 3.

FALLING PROFIT, TENDENCY OF

Political economy, which has until now been unable to explain the law of the tendency of the rate of profit to fall, pointed self-consolingly to the increasing mass of profit, i.e., to the growth of the absolute magnitude of profit, be it for the individual capitalist or for the social capital, but this was also based on mere platitude and speculation.—C. 3.

FALLING RENT

From the relation of ground-rent to interest on money it follows that rent must fall more and more, so that eventually only the wealthiest people can live on rent. Hence the ever greater competition between landowners who do not lease their land to tenants. Ruin of some of these—further accumulation of large landed property.—M.

FREEDMEN

The historical movement which changes the producers into wage-workers appears, on the one hand, as their emancipation from serfdom and from the fetters of the guilds, and this side alone exists for our bourgeois historians. But, on the other hand, these new *freedmen* became sellers of themselves only after they had been robbed of all their own means of production, and of all the guarantee of existence afforded by the old feudal arrangements. And the history of this, their expropriation, is written in the annals of mankind in letters of blood and fire.—C. 1.

FREEDOM

By freedom is meant, under the present bourgeois conditions of production, free trade, free selling and buying. —C. M.

The realm of freedom actually begins only where labor which is determined by necessity and mundane considerations ceases; thus in the very nature of things it lies beyond the sphere of actual material production. Just as the savage must wrestle with nature to satisfy his wants, to maintain and reproduce life, so must civilized man, and he must do so in all social formations and under all possible modes of production. With his development this realm of physical necessity expands as a result of his wants; but, at the same time, the forces of production which satisfy these wants also increase.—C. 3.

FREEDOM, ECONOMIC

Freedom in the economic field can only consist in socialized men, the associated producers, rationally regulating their interchange with nature, bringing it under their common control, instead of being ruled by it as by the blind forces of nature; and achieving this with the least expenditure of energy and under conditions most favorable to, and worthy of, their human nature. Beyond it begins that development of human energy which is an end in itself, the true realm of freedom, which, however, can blossom forth only with this realm of necessity as its basis.—C. 3.

FREEDOM OF CONSCIENCE

Among the human rights is freedom of conscience, the right to practice the religion of one's choice. The privilege of belief is implicitly recognized either as a human right or as a consequence of human rights (freedom).—J. Q.

G

GEOGENY
The creation of the earth has received a mighty blow from *geogeny*—i.e., from the science which presents the formation of the earth, the coming-to-be of the earth, as a process, as self-generation.—M.

GEOLOGY
Geological revolutions have created the surface of the earth.—D. T.

GERMAN BOURGEOISIE
In Germany the petty bourgeois class, a relic of the sixteenth century, and since then constantly cropping up again under various forms, is the real social basis of the existing state of things. To preserve this class is to preserve the existing state of things in Germany.—C. M.

GERMAN INDUSTRY
In German industry, [the] maxim is: People will surely appreciate if we send them good samples first, and then inferior goods afterward.—C. 3.

GERMAN PHILOSOPHY

To the German philosophers of the eighteenth century, the demands of the first French Revolution were nothing more than the demands of "Practical Reason" in general, and the utterance of the will of the revolutionary French bourgeoisie signified in their eyes the laws of pure Will, of Will as it was bound to be, of true human Will generally.—C. M.

GOVERNMENT SECURITIES

Government securities, like stocks and other securities of all kinds, are spheres of investment for loanable capital—capital intended for bearing interest. They are forms of loaning such capital. But they themselves are not the loan capital, which is invested in them.—C. 3.

GRATIFICATION

In what manner the object exists for man's feelings is the characteristic mode of their gratification.—M.

GREECE

Greece and Rome are certainly the countries of the highest "historical culture" among the peoples of antiquity. The peak of Greece's greatest internal progress coincides with the time of Pericles, its external zenith with the time of Alexander.—L. A.

Greek society was founded upon slavery, and had, therefore, for its natural basis, the inequality of men and of their labor powers.—C. 1.

GROUND RENT

Ground rent may in another form be confused with interest and thereby its specific character overlooked. Ground rent assumes the form of a certain sum of money, which the landlord draws annually by leasing a certain plot on our planet.—C. 3.

We have already learnt that the size of the rent depends on the degree of fertility of the land. Another factor in its determination is situation.—M.

The relation between increasing house rent and increasing poverty is an example of the landlord's interest in society, for the ground rent, the interest obtained from the land on which the house stands, goes up with the rent of the house.—M.

In theory, ground rent and profit on capital are deductions suffered by wages.—M.

H

HABITATION, HUMAN
Man returns to living in a cave, which is now, however, contaminated with the mephitic breath of plague given off by civilization, and which he continues to occupy only precariously, it being for him an alien habitation which can be withdrawn from him any day—a place from which, if he does not pay, he can be thrown out any day. For this mortuary he has to pay.—M.

HANDICRAFT SKILL
Handicraft skill is the foundation of manufacture.—C. 1.

HEGEL
I would like to explain to the ordinary human understanding what is rational in the method which Hegel discovered but also wrapped up in mysticism.—Ltr. to Engels.

Hegel has no problems to put. He has only dialectic.—P. P.

One must begin with Hegel's *Phaenomenologie*, the true point of origin and the secret of the Hegelian philosophy.—M.

The outstanding thing in Hegel's *Phaenomenologie* is that Hegel conceives the self-genesis of man as a process, conceives objectification as loss of the object, as alienation and as transcendence of this alienation; that he thus grasps the essence of labor and comprehends objective man—true, because real man—as the outcome of man's own labor.—M.

For Hegel the essence of man—man—equals self-consciousness. All estrangement of the human essence is therefore nothing but estrangement of self-consciousness. The estrangement of self-consciousness is not regarded as an expression of the real estrangement of the human being—its expression reflected in the realm of knowledge and thought. Instead, the real estrangement—that which appears real—is from its innermost, hidden nature (a nature only brought to light by philosophy) nothing but the manifestation of the estrangement of the real essence of man, of self-consciousness. The science which comprehends this is therefore called *Phenomenology*.—M.

Hegel's *Encyclopaedia*, beginning as it does with Logic, with pure speculative thought, and ending with Absolute Knowledge—with the self-consciousness, self-comprehending, philosophic or absolute (i.e., superhuman) abstract mind— is in its entirety nothing but the display, the self-objectification, of the essence of the philosophic mind, and the philosophic mind is nothing but the estranged mind of the world thinking its self-estrangement—i.e., comprehending itself abstractly.—M.

Because Hegel has conceived the negation of the negation from the point of view of the positive relation inherent in it as the true and only positive, and from the point of view of the negative relation inherent in it as the only true act and self-realizing act of all being, he has only found the abstract, logical, speculative expression for the movement of history; and this historical process is not yet the real history of man—of man as a given subject, but only man's act of genesis—the story of man's origin.—M.

Speculative philosophy, that is, Hegel's philosophy, first had to translate all questions from the language of every sound common sense into the language of the speculative intellect and turn every real question into a speculative question before it could answer it.—J. Q.

HEIRS
The heirs are quarreling among themselves over the inheritance even before the obituary notice has been printed and the testament read.—H. P.

HEROISM
Bourgeois society is lacking in heroism.—E. B.

HISTORIC REVERSION
At the very time when men appear engaged in revolutionizing things and themselves, in bringing about what never was before, precisely at such epochs of revolutionary crisis do they anxiously conjure up into their service the spirits of the past, assume their names, their battle cries, their costumes, to enact a new historic scene in such time-honored disguise and with such borrowed language.—E. B.

HISTORICAL FORM
In order to examine the connection between spiritual production and material production it is above all necessary to grasp the latter itself not as a general category but in definite historical form.—C. 4.

HISTORICAL MATERIALISM

The social organization and the state constantly arise from the life-process of definite individuals, of those individuals not as they or other people imagine them to be, but as they are really, i.e., as they act, as they materially produce, consequently as they are active under definite material limitations, provisions and conditions which do not depend on their free will.—G. I.

What avails lamentation in the face of *historical necessity?* —C. 1.

HISTORICAL RECURRENCE

All great historic facts and personages recur twice—once as tragedy, and once as farce.—E. B.

HISTORICAL RETRIBUTION

There is something in human history like retribution; and it is a rule of *historical retribution* that its instrument be forged not by the offended, but by the offender himself.—D. T.

HISTORY

History resembles paleontology. Owing to certain prejudices even the best scientists do not notice facts which lie in front of their noses. Later, they are surprised to discover traces everywhere of what they failed to realize.—Ltr. to Engels.

Human history differs from natural history in this, that we have made the former, but not the latter.—C. 1.

Man makes his own history, but he does not make it out of whole cloth; he does not make it out of conditions chosen by himself, but out of such as he finds close at hand.—E. B.

All history is the preparation for "man" to become the object of sensuous consciousness, and for the needs of "man as man" to become (natural, sensuous) needs. History itself is a real part of natural history—of nature's coming to be man. Natural science will in time subsume under itself the science of man, just as the science of man will subsume under itself natural science.—M.

After philosophy comes history. This is no longer either descriptive history or dialectic history, it is comparative history.—P. P.

All preceding conception of history has either completely ignored the real basis of history or has considered it only as incidental and in no way connected with the course of history. That is why history had always to be written according to a standing lying outside it; real life-production appeared as prehistoric while what was historical appeared as separated from common life and extra-supra-mundane. Man's relation to nature was thus excluded from history, as a result of which the antithesis of nature and history was produced. Hence this conception of history saw in history only the main official actions of the state and the religious and generally theoretical struggles.—G. I.

The entire movement of history is both its actual act of genesis (the birth act of its empirical existence) and also for its thinking consciousness the comprehended and known process of its coming-to-be.—M.

HISTORY, BOURGEOIS
The bourgeois period of history has to create the material basis of the new world—on the one hand the universal intercourse founded upon the mutual dependency of

mankind, and the means of that intercourse; on the other hand the development of the productive powers of man and the transformation of material production into a scientific domination of natural agencies. Bourgeois industry and commerce create these material conditions of a new world in the same way as geological revolutions have created the surface of the earth.—D. T.

HISTORY, MATERIALISTIC CONCEPTION OF

This conception of history has not to seek a category in every epoch like the idealistic conception of history, but it remains constantly on the real ground of history; it does not explain practice by the idea but explains the formation of ideas by material practice. Accordingly it comes to the result that all forms and products of consciousness can be dissolved not by spiritual criticism, but by the practical overthrow of the real social relations; that not criticism but revolution is the motive force of history as well as of religion, philosophy and all other forms of theory.—G. I.

HISTORY, TASK OF

The task of history, once the world beyond the truth has disappeared, is to establish the truth of this world. The immediate task of philosophy, which is at the service of history, once the saintly form of human self-alienation has been unmasked, is to unmask self-alienation in its unholy forms. Thus the criticism of heaven turns into the criticism of the earth, the criticism of religion into the criticism of right and the criticism of theology into the criticism of politics.—C. C.

HOARDING

The simplest form in which the additional latent money-capital may be represented is that of a hoard. It may be that this hoard is additional gold or silver secured directly or indirectly in exchange with countries producing precious metals. And only in this manner does the hoarded money in a country grow absolutely. On the other hand, it may be— and is so in the majority of cases—that this hoard is nothing but money which has been withdrawn from circulation at home and has assumed the form of a hoard in the hands of individual capitalists.—C. 2.

HOBBES
According to Hobbes science, not operative labor, is the mother of the arts. The product of mental labor—science— always stands far below its value, because the labor-time needed to reproduce it has no relation at all to the labor-time for its original production. For example, a schoolboy can learn the binominal theorem in an hour.—C. 4.

For Hobbes labor is the sole source of all wealth, apart from those gifts of nature which are to be found already in a consumable state.—C. 4.

HOME INDUSTRY
The home and petty form of industry is intended for self-consumption, not producing commodities.—C. 4.

HONOR
Honor attaches to great historic struggles.—E. B.

HOSPITALITY
It is a custom in the north to treat guests to exquisite liqueurs before meager meals.—L. A.

HOSTILITY, CAPITALIST
Capitalist production is hostile to certain branches of spiritual production, for example, art and poetry.—C. 4.

The interest of the capitalists, even from the point of view commonly held by political economists, stands in hostile opposition to society.—M.

HOSTILITY, INTERNATIONAL
In proportion as the exploitation of one individual by another is put an end to, the exploitation of one nation by another will also be put an end to. In proportion as the antagonism between classes within the nation vanishes, the hostility of one nation to another will come to an end.—C. M.

HOUSE RENT
House rent stands in inverse proportion to industrial poverty. The lower the standard of living, the higher the house rent.—M.

HUCKSTERING
Feudal landed property is already by its very nature huckstered land.—M.

HUMAN
Assume man to be man and his relationship to the world to be a human one: then you can exchange love only for love, trust for trust, etc.—M.

I

IDEAL SOCIETY
Society in a state of maximum wealth—an ideal.—M.

IDEALISM
Idealism does not know real, sensuous activity as such.—T. F.

IDEOLOGY
Ideology is a process achieved by a so-called thinker, consciously, it is true, but with a false consciousness. He is not aware of his real driving motives—only for this reason it is an ideological process.—Ltr. to Mehring.

Morals, religion, metaphysics and other forms of ideology and the forms of consciousness corresponding to them no longer retain their apparent independence. They have no history, they have no development, but men, developing their material production and their material intercourse, with this, their reality, their thinking and the products of their thinking also change.—G. I.

IDOLATRY
Man debases himself by idolatry.—H. F.

IMPORT TRADE
The volume of import trade is determined and stimulated by the export trade.—C. 2.

IMPOVERISHMENT
The accumulation of wealth at one pole is at the same time accumulation of slavery, ignorance, brutality, mental degradation at the opposite pole, that is, on the side of the class that produces its product.—C. 1.

IMPOVERISHMENT OF THE WORKER
When society is in a state of decline, the worker suffers most severely. The specific severity of his burden he owes to his position as a worker, but the burden as such to the position of society. But when society is in a state of progress, the ruin and impoverishment of the worker is the product of his labor and of the wealth produced by him. The misery results, therefore, from the essence of present-day labor itself.—M.

IMPROVEMENT OF MACHINERY
Improved construction of the machinery is necessary, partly because without it greater pressure cannot be put on the workman, and partly because the shortened hours of labor force the capitalist to exercise the strictest watch over the cost of production. The improvements in the steam-engine have increased the piston speed. . . . The improvements in the transmitting mechanism have lessened friction.—C. 1.

IMPULSES

As a living natural being man is furnished with natural powers of life—he is an active natural being. These forces exist in him as tendencies and abilities—as impulses.—M.

INCREASE IN PRODUCTION

As the use of machinery extends in a given industry, the immediate effect is to increase production in the other industries that furnish the first with means of production.—C. 1.

INDEPENDENCE

A being only considers himself independent when he stands on his own feet; and he only stands on his own feet when he owes his existence to himself.—M.

In bourgeois society capital is independent and has individuality, while the living person is dependent and has no individuality.—C. M.

J

JOBBING TAILOR

The jobbing tailor (who works for me at my home) is not a productive laborer, although his labor provides me with the product, the trousers, and him with the price of his labor, the money. It may be that the quantity of labor performed by the jobbing tailor is greater than that contained in the price which he gets from me. And this is even probable. This however is all the same so far as I am concerned. Once the price has been fixed, it is a matter of complete indifference to me whether he works eight or ten hours. What I am concerned with is only the use-value, the trousers; and naturally, whether I buy them one way or the other, I am interested in paying as little as possible for them, but in one case neither less nor more than in the other; in other words, I am interested in paying only the normal price for them.—C. 4.

JOHN BULL

As Delhi has not, like the walls of Jericho, fallen before mere puffs of wind, John Bull is to be steeped in cries of revenge up to his very ears, to make him forget that this government is responsible for the mischief hatched and the colossal dimensions it had been allowed to assume.—D. T.

It is certain that these obstinate John Bulls, whose skulls appear to have been manufactured for the bludgeons of the constables, will never accomplish anything without a truly bloody struggle with the ruling powers.—Ltr. to Engels.

JUDAISM
Judaism has maintained itself not in spite of, but because of, history.—J. Q.

JUNE INSURRECTION
The Paris proletariat answered with the June Insurrection, the most colossal event in the history of European civil wars.—E. B.

JURIDICAL RELATION
The juridical relation which expresses itself in a contract, whether such contract be part of a developed legal system or not, is a relation between two wills, and is but the reflex of the real economical relation between the two. It is this economical relation that determines the subject-matter comprised in each such juridical act.—C. 1.

JURISPRUDENCE
Your jurisprudence is but the will of your class made into a law for all, a will whose essential character and direction are determined by the economic conditions of existence of your class.—C. M.

JUSTIFICATION, BOURGEOIS
When the spiritual labors themselves are more and more performed in its service and enter into the service of capi-

talist production—then things take a new turn, and the bourgeoisie tries to justify "economically," from its own standpoint, what at an earlier stage it had criticized and fought against. Its spokesmen and conscience-salvers in this line are the Garniers, etc. In addition to this, these economists, who themselves are priests, professors, etc., are eager to prove their "productive" usefulness, to justify their wages "economically."—C. 4.

K

KANT
Kant considers the solution of the antinomies as something "beyond" the human understanding.—Ltr. to Schweitzer.

KNELL OF CAPITALISM
The monopoly of capital becomes a fetter upon the mode of production, which has sprung up and flourished along with it, and under it. Centralization of the means of production and socialization of labor at last reach a point where they become incompatible with their capitalist integument. This integument is burst asunder. The knell of capitalist private property sounds. The expropriators are expropriated.—C. 1.

KOSCIUSKO
Why does the popular dictator Kosciusko tolerate a king beside himself?—Ltr. to Engels.

KUGELMANN
Kugelmann is a fanatical advocate of our doctrine and of us both. He sometimes annoys me with his enthusiasm, which

is at variance with his detachment as a medical man. However, he understands, and is very honest. He also is resolute, self-sacrificing, and, what is the most important, convinced.—Ltr. to Engels.

L

LABOR

Labor is man's active property.—M.

Labor is the source of value.—P. P.

Man enhances through labor the value of the products of nature.—M.

Labor, is in the first place, a process in which both man and nature participate, and in which man of his own accord starts, regulates, and controls the material reactions between himself and nature. He opposes himself to nature as one of her own forces, setting in motion arms and legs, head and hands, the natural forces of his body, in order to appropriate nature's productions in a form adapted to his own wants.—C. 1.

That which determines the magnitude of the value of any article is the amount of labor socially necessary, or the labor-time socially necessary for its production. Each individual commodity, in this connection, is to be considered as an average sample of its class.—C. 1.

LABOR, ABSTRACT

A use-value, or useful article, has value only because human labor in the abstract has been embodied or materialized in it.—C. 1.

LABOR, CAPITALIST

The labor of a capitalist stands altogether in inverse proportion to the size of his capital.—C. 3.

LABOR, CHILD

The capitalist buys children and young persons under age.—C. 1.

LABOR, COMMUNIST

In bourgeois society, living labor is but a means to increase accumulated labor. In communist society, accumulated labor is but a means to widen, to enrich, to promote the existence of the laborer.—C. M.

LABOR, COST OF

The constant tendency of capital is to force the cost of labor back toward zero.—C. 1.

LABOR, ESTRANGEMENT OF

Political economy starts from labor as the real soul of production; yet to labor it gives nothing, and to private property everything. From this contradiction Proudhon has concluded in favor of labor and against private property. We understand, however, that this apparent contradiction is the contradiction of estranged labor with itself, and that political economy has merely formulated the laws of estranged labor.—M.

The laws of political economy express the estrangement of the worker in his object thus: the more the worker produces, the less he has to consume; the more values he creates, the more valueless, the more unworthy he becomes; the better formed his product, the more deformed becomes the worker; the more civilized his object, the more barbarous becomes the worker; the mightier labor becomes, the more powerless becomes the worker; the more ingenious labor becomes, the duller becomes the worker and the more he becomes nature's bondsman.—M.

LABOR, INSTRUMENTS OF
It is not the workman that employs the instruments of labor, but the instruments of labor that employ the workman.—C. 1.

All other circumstances being equal, the degree of fixity increases with the durability of the instrument of labor. It is this durability that determines the magnitude of the difference between the capital-value fixed in instruments of labor and that part of its value which it yields to the product in repeated labor-processes.—C. 2.

LABOR, MEANS OF
The unity (of labor) in cooperation, the combination (of labor) through the division of labor, the use for productive purposes in machine industry of the forces of nature and science alongside the products of labor—all this confronts the individual laborers themselves as something extraneous and objective, as a mere form of existence of the means of labor that are independent of them and control them.—C. 4.

LABOR, MEASUREMENT OF
The quantity of labor is measured by its duration.—C. 1.

LABOR, ORGANIZATION OF
The organization of labor is determined by the means of production.—Ltr. to Engels.

LABOR, PRICE OF
The cost of production of a workman is restricted, almost entirely, to the means of subsistence that he requires for his maintenance, and for the propagation of his race.—C. M.

The price of labor, at the moment when demand and supply are in equilibrium, is its natural price, determined independently of the relation of demand and supply.—C. 1.

LABOR, PRODUCTS OF
It is true that labor produces for the rich wonderful things—but for the worker it produces privation. It produces palaces—but for the worker, hovels. It produces beauty—but for the worker, deformity. It replaces labor by machines—but some of the workers it throws back to a barbarous type of labor, and the other workers it turns into machines. It produces intelligence—but for the worker idiocy, cretinism.—M.

LABOR POWER
By labor power or capacity for labor is to be understood the aggregate of those mental and physical capabilities existing in a human being, which he exercises whenever he produces a use-value of any description.—C. 1.

Human labor power is by nature no more capital than are the means of production.—C. 2.

Simple labor power, on an average, apart from any special development, exists in the organism of every ordinary individual.—C. 1.

The value of labor power is determined by the labor-time necessary for the reproduction of this special article.—C. 1.

LABOR POWER, CONSUMPTION OF
The consumption of labor power is at one and the same time the production of commodities and of surplus-value. The consumption of labor power is completed, as in the case of every other commodity, outside the limits of the market or of the sphere of circulation.—C. 1.

LABOR POWER, EXHAUSTION OF
The capitalistic mode of production (essentially the production of surplus-value, the absorption of surplus-labor), produces thus, with the extension of the working day, not only the deterioration of human labor power by robbing it of its normal, moral and physical conditions of development and function. It produces also the premature exhaustion and death of this labor power itself. It extends the laborer's time of production during a given period by shortening his actual lifetime.—C. 1.

LABOR POWER, PURCHASE OF
By the purchase of labor power, the capitalist incorporates labor, as a living ferment, with the lifeless constituents of the product. From his point of view, the labor-process is nothing more than the consumption of the commodity purchased, i.e., of labor power.—C. 1.

The capitalist buys labor power in order to use it; and labor power in use is labor itself. The purchaser of labor power consumes it by setting the seller of it to work. By working, the latter becomes actually, what before he only was potentially, labor power in action, a laborer.—C. 1.

LASSALLE

It is the immortal achievement of Lassalle to have reawakened the German workers' movement after its fifteen years of slumber. He however committed serious mistakes; he allowed himself to be too much guided by the nearest circumstances of his time.—Ltr. to Schweitzer.

Lassalle went astray because he was a "Realpolitiker."—Ltr. to Kugelmann.

Lassalle, dazzled by the reputation he enjoys in certain scholarly circles by his *Heraclitus* and in a certain group of parasites by his excellent wine and cookery, is unaware of his discredit among the community at large. There also is his mania to be always right, his adherence to Hegel's "speculative conception," his infection with old French liberalism, his inflated writing, his importunity, tactlessness, etc.—Ltr. to Engels.

The moment Lassalle was convinced that he could not play his games with me, he decided to establish himself as the "workers'" dictator against me.—Ltr. to Kugelmann.

Heraclitus the Dark by *Lassalle* the Bright basically is a very silly bungling work.—Ltr. to Engels.

Lassalle's misfortune has been damnably in my head these days. After all he was still one of the old guard and the adversary of our adversaries. And then the thing happened so surprisingly that it is hard to believe such a noisy, stirring, pushing man is now as dead as a mouse and has got to keep his mouth shut altogether.—Ltr. to Engels.

LAW, CIVIL
Are not the majority of civil laws concerned with property?—L. A.

LAW OF CAPITALIST PRODUCTION
The law of capitalist production, that is at the bottom of the pretended "natural law of population," reduces itself simply to this: The correlation between accumulation of capital and rate of wages is nothing else than the correlation between the unpaid labor transformed into capital, and the additional paid labor necessary for the setting in motion of this additional capital. It is therefore in no way a relation between two magnitudes, independent one of the other: on the one hand, the magnitude of the capital; on the other, the number of the laboring population; it is rather, at bottom, only the relation between unpaid and the paid labor of the same laboring population.—C. 1.

LAW OF CAPITALISTIC ACCUMULATION
The law of capitalistic accumulation, metamorphosed by economists into a pretended law of nature, in reality merely states that the very nature of accumulation excludes every diminution in the degree of exploitation of labor, and every rise in the price of labor, which could seriously imperil the continual reproduction, on an ever enlarging scale, of the capitalistic relation.—C. 1.

LAW OF CIRCULATION OF COMMODITIES
According to the law of the circulation of commodities, the quantity of money must be equal to the amount of money required for circulation plus a certain amount held in the

form of a hoard, which increases or decreases as the circulation contracts or expands.—C. 1.

LAW OF FALLING PROFIT
The law of the falling rate of profit, which expresses the same, or even a higher, rate of surplus-value, states that any quantity of the average social capital, say, a capital of 100, comprises an ever larger portion of means of labor, and an ever smaller portion of living labor.—C. 3.

LAW OF INCREASING PROLETARIAN MISERY
Along with the constantly diminishing number of the magnates of capital grows the mass of misery.—C. 1.

LAW OF POPULATION
Every historic mode of (human) production has its own special laws of population. An abstract law of population exists for plants and animals only insofar as man has not interfered with them.—C. 1.

M

MACHINE AND TOOL
There is a great dispute as to what distinguishes a machine from a tool. The English merchants, in their crude manner, denote a tool a simple machine and a machine a complicated tool. The English technologists, however, base the distinction between the two on the fact that in one case the motive power originates from a human being, in the other from a natural force. The German asses, who are great at these small affairs, have therefore concluded that, for instance, a plough is a machine, while the most complicated spinning-jenny, etc., insofar as it is worked by hand, is not.—Ltr. to Engels.

MACHINE COMPETITION
Every article produced by a machine is cheaper than a similar article by hand.—C. 1.

The division of labor brings with it the competition not only of men but of machines. Since the worker has sunk to the level of a machine, he can be confronted by the machine as a competitor.—M.

MACHINE LABOR

As long as the labor spent on a machine, and consequently the portion of its value added to the product, remains smaller than the value added by the workman to the product with his tool, there is always a difference of labor saved in favor of the machine. The productiveness of a machine is therefore measured by the human labor power it replaces.—C. 1.

MANUFACTORY

A manufactory consists in the union of a large number of work-people and many varied trades in a single place, in one apartment, under the control of one capital, than in the analysis of the different operations and the adaptation of each worker to one simple task.—P. P.

MANUFACTURE

The feudal system of industry, under which industrial production was monopolized by closed guilds, no longer sufficed for the growing wants of the markets. The manufacturing system took its place.—C. M.

Manufacture either introduces division of labor into a process of production, or further develops that division; on the other hand, it unites together handicrafts that were formerly separate. But whatever may have been its particular starting point, its final form is invariably the same—a productive mechanism whose parts are human beings.—C. 1.

Manufacture is characterized by the differentiation of the instruments of labor—a differentiation whereby implements of a given sort acquire fixed shapes, adapted to each particular application, and by the specialization of those instruments, giving to each special instrument its full play only in the hands of a specific detail laborer.—C. 1.

With regard to the mode of production itself, manufacture, in its strict meaning, is hardly to be distinguished, in its earliest stages, from the handicraft trades of the guilds, otherwise than by the greater number of workmen simultaneously employed by one and the same individual capital. The workshop of the medieval master handicraftsman is simply enlarged.—C. 1.

While simple cooperation leaves the mode of working by the individual for the most part unchanged, manufacture thoroughly revolutionizes it, and seizes labor power by its roots. It converts the laborer into a crippled monstrosity, by forcing his detail dexterity at the expense of a world of productive capabilities and instincts.—C. 1.

The advance made by human labor in converting the product of nature into the manufactured product of nature increases, not the wages of labor, but in part the number of profitable capitals, and in part the size of every subsequent capital in comparison with the foregoing.—M.

MANUFACTURING PERIOD
The manufacturing period simplifies, improves, and multiplies the implements of labor, by adapting them to the exclusively special functions of each detail laborer. It thus creates at the same time one of the material conditions for the existence of machinery, which consists of a combination of simple instruments.—C. 1.

MANUFACTURING SECRETS
The capitalist gains by virtue of some manufacturing or trading secret.—M.

The worker need not necessarily gain when the capitalist does, but he necessarily loses when the latter loses. Thus the worker does not gain if the capitalist keeps the market-price above the natural price by virtue of some manufacturing or trading secret, or by virtue of monopoly or the favorable situation of his property.—M.

MARGINAL DETERMINATION
If the supply is too small, the market-value is always regulated by the commodities produced under the least favorable circumstances and, if the supply is too large, always by the commodities produced under the most favorable conditions: it is one of the extremes which determines the market-value.—C. 3.

MARKET
The transaction in the market effectuates only the interchange of the individual components of the annual product, transfers them from one hand to another, but can neither augment the total annual production nor alter the nature of the objects produced.—C.1.

MARKET, INTERNATIONAL
The need of a constantly expanding market for its products chases the bourgeoisie over the whole surface of the globe. It must nestle everywhere, settle everywhere, establish connections everywhere.—C. M.

MARKET PRICE
The market price signifies that the same price is paid for commodities of the same kind, although they may have been produced under very different individual conditions and hence may have considerably different cost prices.—C. 3.

MARRIAGE

Bourgeois marriage is in reality a system of wives in common and thus, at the most, what the communists might possibly be reproached with is that they desire to introduce, in substitution for a hypocritically concealed, an openly legalized community of women.—C. M.

MARX AT WORK

I am now working like a horse, because I must use the time in which it is possible to work and the carbuncles are still there though now they only disturb me locally and not in the cranium. Between whiles, since one cannot always be writing, I am doing some Differential Calculus. I have no patience to read anything else. Any other reading drives me back to my writing desk.—Ltr. to Engels.

Because of its gigantic shape the manuscript, although finished, cannot be completed for publication by anyone but me, not even by you. The thing progressed very quickly, since it naturally is intriguing to lick the baby smooth after so many birth pangs. However, the carbuncle again interfered, so that I could not really proceed. And to finish the work, I must at least be able to sit down.—Ltr. to Engels.

Dear Fred: I have just finished correcting the last sheet of the book. Preface ditto corrected and returned yesterday. So this volume is finished. This has been possible thanks to *you* alone. Without your self-sacrifice for me I could never possibly have accomplished the enormous preparations of the three volumes. I embrace you, full of thanks!
Enclosed two sheets of corrected proofs.
The £ 15 received with best thanks.
Greetings, my dear, beloved friend!
Yours,
K. Marx—Ltr. to Engels.

MATERIALISM

The materialist doctrine that men are products of circumstances and upbringing, and that, therefore, changed men are products of other circumstances and changed upbringing, forgets that it is men that change circumstances and that the educator himself needs educating.—T. F.

The chief defect of all hitherto existing materialism is that the thing, reality, sensuousness, is conceived only in the form of the object or of sensuous perception, but not as human sensuous activity, practice, not subjectively.—H. F.

The standpoint of the old materialism is "civil" society; the standpoint of the new is human society, or socialized humanity.—T. F.

MATERIALISM, BRITISH

Materialism is the native son of Great Britain. Even Britain's scholastic Duns Scotus wondered: "Can matter think?"—H. F.

MATERIALISM, DIALECTICAL

In direct opposition to German philosophy, which comes down from heaven to earth, here there is ascension from earth to heaven. That means that we proceed not from what men say, fancy or imagine, nor from men as they are spoken of, thought, fancied, imagined in order to arrive from them at men of flesh and blood; we proceed from the really active men and see the development of the ideological reflexes and echoes of their real life-process as proceeding from that life-process. Even the nebulous images in the brains of men are necessary sublimates of their material, empirically observable, materially preconditioned life-process.—G. I.

MATERIALISM, HISTORICAL

The production of notions, ideas and consciousness is from the beginning directly interwoven with the material activity and the material intercourse of human beings, the language of real life. The production of men's ideas, thinking, their spiritual intercourse, here appear as the direct efflux of their material condition. The same applies to spiritual production as represented in the language of politics, laws, morals, religion, metaphysics, etc. of a people. The producers of men's ideas, notions, etc., are men, but real active men as determined by a definite development of the productive forces and the intercourse corresponding to those productive forces up to its remotest form.—G. I.

What else does the history of ideas prove than that intellectual production changes in character in proportion as material production is changed? The ruling ideas of each age have ever been the ideas of the ruling class.—C. M.

Does it require deep intuition to comprehend that man's ideas, views, and conceptions, in one word, man's consciousness, change with every change in the condition of his material existence, in his social relations and in his social life?—C. M.

Different kinds of spiritual production correspond to the capitalist mode of production and to the mode of production of the Middle Ages. If material production itself is not conceived in its specific historical form, it is impossible to understand what is specific in the spiritual production corresponding to it.—C. 4.

MATERIALISM AND COMMUNISM

There is no need of any great penetration to see from the

teaching of materialism on the original goodness and equal intellectual endowment of men, the omnipotence of experience, habit and education, and the influence of environment on man, the great significance of industry, the justification of enjoyment, etc., how necessarily materialism is connected with communism and socialism.—H. F.

MATERIALISTIC DETERMINISM
It is not consciousness that determines life, but life that determines consciousness. In the first view one proceeds from consciousness as from the living individual; in the second, in conformity with real life, from the real living individuals themselves, considering consciousness only as *their* consciousness.—G. I.

MATERIALISTIC UNDERSTRUCTURE (Unterbau)
The sum of productive forces, capitals and forms of social intercourse which every individual and every generation finds already in existence is the real basis of what the philosophers imagined to be the "substance" and "essence of man," what they apotheosized and fought against, a real basis which is not in the least disturbed in its action and influence on the development of man by those philosophers, as "self-consciousness" and "ego," rebelling against it.—G. I.

MEANS OF LIFE
Nature provides labor with the means of life in the sense that labor cannot live without objects on which to operate.—M.

MEANS OF PRODUCTION
In a capitalist society, the laborer does not employ the means of production, but the means of production employ the laborer.—C. 1.

MEANS OF SUBSISTENCE
Some of the means of subsistence, such as food and fuel, are consumed daily, and a fresh supply must be provided daily. Others such as clothes and furniture last for longer periods and require to be replaced only at longer intervals. . . . But in whatever way the sum total of these outlays may be spread over the year, they must be covered by the average income, taking one day with another.—C. 1.

MECHANISM OF MANUFACTURE
By decomposition of handicrafts, by specialization of the instruments of labor, by the formation of detail laborers, and by grouping and combining the latter into a single mechanism, division of labor in manufacture creates a qualitative graduation, and a quantitative proportion in the social process of production; it consequently creates a definite organization of the labor of society, and thereby develops at the same time new productive forces in the society.—C. 1.

MERCANTILE SYSTEM
Production and consumption are essentially inseparable. From this it follows that since in the system of capitalist production they are in fact separated, their unity is restored through their opposition—that if A must produce for B, B must consume for A. Just as we find with every individual capitalist that he favors prodigality on the part of those who are co-partners with him in his revenue, so the older mercantile system as a whole depends on the idea that a nation must be frugal as regards itself, but must produce luxuries for foreign nations to enjoy. The idea here is always: on the one side, production for production, therefore on the other side consumption of foreign production.—C.4.

MERCENARY TROOPS

Mercenary troops on a large scale appeared first among the Carthaginians.—Ltr. to Engels.

MERCHANTS CAPITAL

Merchant's, or trading, capital breaks up into two forms or subdivisions, namely, commercial capital and money-dealing capital, which we shall now define more closely, insofar as this is necessary for our analysis of capital in its basic structure. This is all the more necessary because modern political economy, even in the persons of its best exponents, throws trading capital and industrial capital indiscriminately together and, in effect, wholly overlooks the characteristic peculiarities of the former.—C. 3.

The turnover of merchant's capital is not identical with the turnover, or a single reproduction, of an industrial capital of equal size; it is rather equal to the sum of the turnovers of a number of such capitals, whether in the same or in different spheres of production. The more quickly merchant's capital is turned over, the smaller the portion of total money-capital serving as merchant's capital; and conversely, the more slowly it is turned over, the larger this portion.—C. 3.

The great economists are perplexed over mercantile capital being a special variety, since they consider the basic form of capital, capital as industrial capital, and circulation capital (commodity-capital and money-capital) solely because it is a phase in the reproduction process of every capital. The rules concerning the formation of value, profit, etc., immediately deduced by them from their study of industrial capital, do not extend directly to merchant's capital. For this reason, they leave merchant's capital entirely aside and mention it only as a kind of industrial capital. Wherever they make a special analysis of it, they seek to demonstrate that it creates no value.—C. 3.

MERGER
It is concentration of capitals already formed, destruction of their individual independence, expropriation of capitalist by capitalist, transformation of many small into few large capitals.—C. 1.

MONEY
Money itself has no price.—C. 1.

Man becomes ever poorer as man; his need for money becomes ever greater if he wants to overpower hostile beings; and the power of his money declines exactly in inverse proportion to the increase in the volume of production.—M.

Money is the alienated ability of mankind. That which I am unable to do as man, and of which therefore all my individual essential powers are incapable, I am able to do by means of money. Money thus turns each of these powers into something which in itself it is not—turns it, that is, into its contrary.—M.

MONEY CAPITAL
Capital in the form of money must always be available, particularly for the payment of wages, before production can be carried on capitalistically—C. 2.

If we conceive society as being not capitalistic but communistic, there will be no money capital at all in the first place, nor the disguises cloaking the transactions arising on account of it.—C. 2.

MONEY-LENDER
The interest of the money-lender in the spendthrift is by no means identical with the interest of the spendthrift.—M.

MONOPOLY
The necessary result of competition is the accumulation of capital in a few hands, and thus the restoration of monopoly in a more terrible form.—M.

The capitalist gains by virtue of monopoly.—M.

Monopoly in all its dreary monotony invades the world of commodities, as, in the sight and to the knowledge of everybody, monopoly invades the world of the instruments of production.—P. P.

The first abolition of monopoly is always its generalization, the broadening of its existence. The abolition of monopoly once it has come to exist in its utmost breadth and inclusiveness is its total annihilation.—M.

Modern monopoly, bourgeois monopoly, is synthetic monopoly, the negation of the negation, the unity of contraries. It is monopoly in its pure, normal, rational state.—P. P.

MONOPOLY PRICES
Monopoly prices are as high as possible.—M.

MORALE, GERMAN
The main stem of German morale and honesty, of the classes as well as of individuals, is rather that modest egoism which asserts its limitedness and allows it to be asserted against itself.—C. C.

MULTILATERAL ACCUMULATION
The formation of many capitals is only possible as a result of multilateral accumulation, since capital comes into being only by accumulation; and multilateral accumulation necessarily turns into unilateral accumulation. Competition among capitals increases accumulation of capitals.—M.

MUTILATION
The infamous mutilations committed by the sepoys remind one of the practices of the Christian Byzantine Empire, or the prescriptions of Emperor Charles V's criminal law, or the English punishments for high treason, as still recorded by Judge Blackstone.—D. T.

MUTINY
A motley crew of mutineering soldiers who have murdered their own officers, torn asunder the ties of discipline, and not succeeded in discovering a man upon whom to bestow the supreme command are certainly the body least likely to organize a serious and protracted resistance.—D. T.

N

NAPOLEON

Napoleon brought about, within France, the conditions under which alone free competition could develop, the partitioned lands be exploited, the nation's unshackled powers of industrial production be utilized; while, beyond the French frontier, he swept away everywhere the establishments of feudality, so far as requisite, to furnish the bourgeois social system of France with fit surroundings of the European continent.—E. B.

NASSAU, WILLIAM, SR.

According to Nassau, doctors should only be paid insofar as they cure, and lawyers insofar as they win lawsuits, and soldiers insofar as they are victorious.—C. 4.

NATIONALISM

In proportion as capitalist production is developed in a country, in the same proportion do the national intensity and productivity of labor there rise above the international level—C. 1.

NATIONALITY

National differences, and antagonisms between peoples, are daily more and more vanishing, owing to the development of the bourgeoisie, to freedom of commerce, to the world market, to uniformity in the mode of production and in the conditions of life corresponding thereto.—C. M.

In the national struggles of the different countries, the communists point out and bring to the front the common interests of the entire proletariat independently of all nationality.—C. M.

NATURAL FORCES

Apart from the natural substances, it is possible to incorporate in the productive process natural forces, which do not cost anything, to act as agents with more or less heightened effect. The degree of their effectiveness depends on methods and scientific developments which cost the capitalist nothing.—C. 2.

NATURAL LAWS

Natural laws cannot be set aside.—Ltr. to Kugelmann.

NATURAL NECESSITY

The true realm of freedom can blossom forth only with the natural realm of necessity as its basis.—C. 3.

NATURAL SCIENCE

The natural sciences have developed an enormous activity and have accumulated a constantly growing mass of material. Philosophy, however, has remained just as alien to them as they remain to philosophy.—M.

NATURE
Nature is man's inorganic body—nature, that is, insofar as it is not itself the human body.—M.

Nature is only the form of the idea's other-being.—M.

The worker can create nothing without nature, without the sensuous external world. It is the material on which his labor is manifested, in which it is active, from which and by means of which it produces.—M.

From the specific form of material production arises a specific relation of men to nature.—C. 4.

Just as plants, animals, stones, the air, etc., constitute a part of human consciousness in the realm of theory, partly as objects of natural science, partly as objects of art—his spiritual inorganic nature, spiritual nourishment which he must first prepare to make it palatable and digestible—so too in the realm of practice they constitute a part of human life and human activity.—M.

NINETEENTH-CENTURY REVOLUTION
The social revolution of the nineteenth century cannot draw its poetry from the past, it can draw that only from the future. It cannot start upon its work before it has stricken off all superstition concerning the past. Former revolutions required historic reminiscences in order to intoxicate themselves with their own content. The revolution of the nineteenth century must let the dead bury their dead in order to achieve its proper content. With the former, the phrase surpasses the content; with the latter, the content surpasses the phrase.—E. B.

NOBILITY AND PROPERTY

The feudal lord does not try to extract the utmost advantage from his land. Rather, he consumes what is there and calmly leaves the worry of producing to the serfs and the tenants. Such is nobility's relationship to landed property, which casts a romantic glory on its lords.—M.

It is necessary that the romantic glory of nobility be abolished—that landed property, the root of private property, be dragged completely into the movement of private property and that it become a commodity; that the rule of the proprietor appear as the undisguised rule of private property, of capital, freed of all political tincture; that the relationship between proprietor and worker be reduced to the economic relationship of exploiter and exploited; that all personal relationship between the proprietor and his property cease, property becoming merely objective, material wealth; that the marriage of convenience should take the place of the marriage of honor with the land; and that the land should likewise sink to the status of a commercial value, like man.—M.

NOMAD RACES

Nomad races are the first to develop the money form, because all their worldly goods consist of movable objects and are therefore directly alienable; and because their mode of life, by continually bringing them into contact with foreign communities, solicits the exchange of products.—C .1

Amongst nomadic peoples it is the horse which makes me a free man and a participant in the life of the community.—M.

O

OBJECTIFICATION
The product of labor is labor which has been congealed in an object: it is the objectification of labor. Labor's realization is its objectification.—M.

OBJECTIVISM, SOCIOLOGICAL
The object as being for man, as the objective being of man for other men, is at the same time the existence of man for other men, his human relation to other men, the social behavior of man in relation to man.—H. F.

OBSERVATION
Observation must reveal the connection of the social and political organization with production.—G. I.

OBSOLETE SOCIAL FORCES
It is an old and historically established maxim that obsolete social forces, nominally still in possession of all the attributes of power and continuing to vegetate long after the basis of their existence has rotted away, inasmuch as the heirs are quarreling among themselves over the inheritance

even before the obituary notice has been printed and the testament read—that these forces once more summon all their strength before their agony of death, pass from the defensive to the offensive, challenge instead of giving way, and seek to draw the most extreme conclusions from premises which have not only been put in question but already condemned.—H. P.

OCCUPATION
All these illustrative and time-honored occupations—sovereign, judge, officer, priest, etc.,—with all the old ideological professions to which they give rise, their men of letters, their teachers and priests, are from an economical standpoint put on the same level as the swarm of their own lackeys and jesters maintained by the bourgeoisie and by idle wealth—the landed nobility and idle capitalists. They are mere servants of the public, just as the others are their servants. They live on the produce of other people's industry, therefore, they must be reduced to the smallest number.—C. 4.

OFFER
A demand is at the same time an offer, an offer is at the same time a demand.—P. P.

OPINION
Our opinion of an individual is not based on what he thinks of himself.—P. E.

OPPOSITION OF INTEREST
Whilst the interest of the worker never stands opposed to the interest of society, society always and necessarily stands opposed to the interest of the worker.—M.

OPPRESSION
Hitherto, every form of society has been based on the antagonism of oppressing and oppressed classes.—C. M.

OPTIMISM, BOURGEOIS
The bourgeoisie naturally conceives the world in which it is supreme to be the best; and bourgeois socialism develops this comfortable conception into various more or less complete systems. In requiring the proletariat to carry out such a system, and thereby to march into the social New Jerusalem, it but requires in reality that the proletariat should remain within the bounds of existing society, but should cast away all its hateful ideas concerning the bourgeoisie.—C. M.

ORATOR
It is true that in our modern parliaments, a part lacking neither dignity nor interest might be imagined of an independent orator who, while despairing of influencing the actual course of events, should content himself to assume a position of ironical neutrality.—D. T.

ORGANIZATION OF LABOR
It is very characteristic that the enthusiastic apologists of the factory system have nothing more damning to urge against a general organization of the labor of society than that it would turn all society into one immense factory.—C. 1.

ORGANS
The organs of plants and animals serve as instruments of production for sustaining life.—C. 1.

ORIENTAL AGRICULTURE
Climate and territorial conditions, especially the vast tracts

of desert, extending from the Sahara, through Arabia, Persia, India and Tartary, to the most elevated Asiatic highlands, constituted artificial irrigation by canals and waterworks the basis of Oriental agriculture.—D. T.

ORIGINAL SIN

Original sin is at work everywhere. As the capitalist production, accumulation, and wealth become developed, the capitalist ceases to be the mere incarnation of capital. He has a fellow-feeling for his own Adam, and his education gradually enables him to smile at the rage for asceticism, as a mere prejudice of the old-fashioned miser.—C. 1.

OUTBIDDING

If the demand for a particular kind of commodity is greater than the supply, one buyer outbids another—within certain limits—and so raises the price of the commodity for all of them above the market-value, while on the other hand the sellers unite in trying to sell at a high market-price.—C. 3.

OUTRAGES, HUMAN

The outrages committed by the revolting sepoys in India are indeed appalling, hideous, ineffable—such as one is prepared to meet only in wars of insurrection, of nationalities, of races, and above all of religions; in one word, such as respectable England used to applaud when perpetrated by the Vendeans on the "Blues," by the Spanish guerrillas on the infidel Frenchmen, by Serbians on their German and Hungarian neighbors, by Croats on Viennese rebels, by Cavaignac's Garde Mobile or Bonaparte's Decembrists on the sons and daughters of proletarian France.—D. T.

OVERPOPULATION

It is no contradiction that overproduction of capital is accompanied by more or less overpopulation. The circumstances which increased the productiveness of labor augmented the mass of produced commodities, expanded markets, accelerated accumulation of capital both in terms of its mass and its value, and lowered the rate of profit—these same circumstances have also created, and continuously create, a relative overpopulation, an overpopulation of laborers not employed by the surplus-capital owing to the low degree of exploitation at which alone they could be employed, or at least owing to the low rate of profit which they would yield at the given degree of exploitation.—C. 3.

Needlessness as the principle of political economy is most brilliantly shown in its theory of population. There are too many people. Even the existence of men is a pure luxury; and if the worker is "ethical," he will be sparing in procreation.—M.

OVERPRODUCTION

In the commercial crises there breaks out an epidemic that, in all earlier epochs, would have seemed an absurdity—the epidemic of overproduction. Society suddenly finds itself put back into a state of momentary barbarism; it appears as if a famine, a universal war of devastation, had cut off the supply of every means of subsistence; industry and commerce seem to be destroyed; and why? Because there is too much civilization, too much means of subsistence, too much industry, too much commerce.—C. M.

P

PAPER MONEY
The state puts in circulation bits of paper on which their various denominations are printed. Insofar as they actually take the place of gold to the same amount, their movement is subject to the laws that regulate the currency of money itself. A law peculiar to the circulation of paper money can spring up only from the proportion in which that paper money represents gold.—C. 1.

PARISIANS
The Parisians manifest adaptability, remarkable initiative, and willingness to sacrifice. After nearly six months of starvation, they revolt. This heroism is unparalleled in history. Only their "good nature" is to be blamed for possible defeat.—Ltr. to Kugelmann.

PARLIAMENTARY ELOQUENCE
Mr. Disraeli's speeches are not intended to carry his motions, but his motions are intended to prepare for his speeches. They might be called self-denying motions, since they are so constructed as neither to harm the adversary, if

carried, nor to damage the proposer, if lost. They mean, in fact, to be neither carried nor lost, but simply to be dropped. They belong neither to the acids nor to the alkalis, but are born neutrals. The speech is not the vehicle of action, but the hypocrisy of action affords the opportunity for a speech. Such, indeed, may be the classical and final form of parliamentary eloquence; but then, at all events, the final form of parliamentary eloquence must not demur to sharing the fate of all final forms of parliamentarism—that of being ranged under the category of nuisances.—D. T.

PLANT
The plant is an object of the sun, being an expression of the life-awakening power of the sun.—M.

PLAY
The care-burdened man in need has no sense for the finest play.—M.

PLEASURE
Pleasure is subsumed under capital, and the pleasure-taking individual under the capital-accumulating individual, whilst formerly the contrary was the case.—M.

PLETHORA, DOUBLE
The plethora of capital arises from the same causes as those which call forth relative overpopulation, and is, therefore, a phenomenon supplementing the latter, although they stand at opposite poles—unemployed capital at one pole, and unemployed worker population at the other.—C. 3.

PLUNDERING
Every new product represents a new potency of mutual swindling and mutual plundering.—M.

POLAND
Poland is the "foreign" thermometer of the intensity and vitality of all revolutions since 1789.—Ltr. to Engels.

POLEMIC
Your article is excellent, both brutal and subtle—a combination which should characterize any polemic worth its salt.—Ltr. to Weydemeyer.

POLITICAL ADVANCE OF THE BOURGEOISIE
Each step in the development of the bourgeoisie was accompanied by a corresponding political advance of that class. An oppressed class under the sway of the feudal nobility, it became an armed and self-governing association in the medieval commune; here an independent urban republic (as in Italy and Germany), there a taxable "third estate" of the monarchy (as in France), afterward, in the period of manufacturing proper, serving either the semi-feudal or the absolute monarchy as a counterpoise against the nobility, and in fact, cornerstone of the great monarchies in general, the bourgeoisie has at last, since the establishment of modern industry and of the world market, conquered for itself, in the modern representative state, exclusive political sway.—C. M.

POLITICAL ECONOMIST
The political economist is an ideological representative of the capitalist.—C. 1.

POLITICAL ECONOMY
Political economy is an independent science.—C. 1.

Political economy—despite its worldly and wanton appearance—is a true *moral* science, the most moral of all sciences.

Self-denial, the denial of life and of all human needs, is its cardinal doctrine. The less you eat, drink and read books— the greater becomes your treasure.—M.

One can transform political economy into a positive science only by substituting real contradictions for conflicting dogmas and conflicting facts whose concealed background they are.—Ltr. to Engels.

Political economy, this science of wealth, is simultaneously the science of denial, of want, of thrift, of saving—and it actually reaches the point where it spares man the need of either fresh air or physical exercise. This science of marvelous industry is simultaneously the science of asceticism, and its true ideal is the ascetic but extortionate miser and the ascetic but productive slave. Its moral ideal is the worker who takes part of his wages to the savings-bank.—M.

Political economy knows the worker only as a working-animal—as a beast reduced to the strictest bodily needs.—M.

Originally, political economy was studied by philosophers like Hobbes, Locke, Hume; by businessmen and statesmen; and especially, and with the greatest success, by medical men. Even in the middle of the eighteenth century, the Rev. Mr. Tucker, a notable economist of his time, excused himself for meddling with the things of mammon. Later on, struck the hour of the Protestant parsons.—C. 1.

Political economy has analyzed, however incompletely, value and its magnitude, and has discovered what lies beneath these forms. But it has never once asked the question why labor is represented by the value of its product and labor-time by the magnitude of that value.—C. 1.

Political economy does not disclose the source of the division between labor and capital, and between capital and land. When, for example, it defines the relationship of wages to profit, it takes the interest of the capitalists to be the ultimate cause; i.e., it takes for granted what it is supposed to evolve.—M.

As to how far external and apparently fortuitous circumstances are but the expression of a necessary course of development political economy teaches us nothing.—M.

The foundation of modern political economy, whose business is the analysis of capitalist production, is the conception of the value of labor power as something fixed, as a given magnitude—as indeed it is in practice in each particular case.—C. 4.

Political economy proceeds from the fact of private property, but it does not explain it to us. It expresses in general, abstract formulae the material process through which private property actually passes, and these formulae it then takes for laws. It does not comprehend these laws—i.e., it does not demonstrate how they arise from the very nature of private property.—M.

POLITICAL MOVEMENT
A political movement is that in which the proletarians as a class exert pressure against the ruling classes. For example, the attempt of the workers of a factory to shorten the working day by a strike simply is an economic movement. However, their attempt at the legislation of an eight-hour day is a political movement.—Ltr. to Bolte.

POLITICAL TRAINING

When the proletariat is not organized enough to conduct a successful struggle against the political power of the ruling class, it must be trained for such a purpose by steady and hostile instigation. Or else, it shall be only a toy in the hands of the bourgeoisie.—Ltr. to Bolte.

POPULATION

Needlessness as the principle of political economy is most brilliantly shown in its theory of population. There are too many people. Even the existence of men is a pure luxury.—M.

Capitalist production collects the population in great centers, and causes an ever-increasing preponderance of the town population.—C. 1.

POPULATION, LABORING

The laboring population produces, along with the accumulation of capital produced by it, the means by which it is made relatively superfluous, is turned into a relative surplus population; and it does this to an always increasing extent. This is a law of population peculiar to the capitalist mode of production; and in fact every special historic mode of production has its own special laws of population, historically valid within its limits alone.—C. 1.

POPULATION DENSITY

The bourgeoisie keeps more and more doing away with the scattered state of the population.—C. M.

POSSESSION

Private property has made us so stupid and one-sided that an object is only *ours* when we have it—when it exists for us as capital, or when it is directly possessed, eaten, drunk, worn, inhabited. etc.—in short, when it is used by us.—M.

POVERTY
Poverty is the passive bond which causes the human being to experience the need of the greatest wealth—the other human being.—M.

In a society based upon poverty, the poorest products have the fatal prerogative of serving the use of the greatest number.—P. P.

POWER, CAPITALIST
The capitalist possesses power, not on account of his personal qualities, but inasmuch as he is an owner of capital.—M.

POWER, PERSONAL
Each person tries to establish over the other an alien power, so as thereby to find satisfaction of his own selfish need. The increase in the quantity of objects is accompanied by an extension of the realm of the alien powers to which man is subjected.—M.

POWER, POLITICAL
Political power, properly so called, is merely the organized power of one class for suppressing another.—C. M.

PRACTICAL SOLUTIONS
It will be seen how subjectivism and objectivism, spiritualism and materialism, activity and suffering, only lose their antithetical character, and thus their existence, as such antitheses in the social condition; it will be seen how the resolution of the theoretical antitheses is only possible in a

practical way, by virtue of the practical energy of men. Their resolution is therefore by no means merely a problem of knowledge, but a real problem of life, which philosophy could not solve precisely because it conceived this problem as merely a theoretical one.—M.

PRACTICE, HUMAN
Social life is essentially practical. All mysteries which mislead theory to mysticism find their rational solution in human practice and in the comprehension of this practice.—T. F.

PREJUDICES, BOURGEOIS
Law, morality, religion, are to the proletarian so many bourgeois prejudices, behind which lurk in ambush just as many bourgeois interests.—C. M.

PRESS, FREEDOM OF THE
The point is whether what lives in reality belongs to the realm of the press; it is no longer a question of a particular content of the press, the question is the general one whether the press must be really the press, i.e., a free press.—L. A.

While the Constitution of 1793 guaranteed *"la liberté indefinie de la presse"* ("unabridged freedom of the press") as a consequence of the right of individual freedom, in reality freedom of the press was completely abolished, for "freedom of the press must not be permitted when it compromises public liberty" (Robespierre).—J. Q.

PRICE
Price is the monetary expression of the relative value of a product.—P. P.

Price is the money-name of the labor realized in a commodity.—C.1.

The price of a commodity, and also of labor, is equal to its cost of production.—C. M.

PRICE, GRAVITATION OF
The market-price gravitates toward the natural price as the center-point.—M.

PRICE INCREASE
A price increase cuts the demand.—C. 3.

PRICE OF LABOR
Classical political economy borrowed from everyday life the category "price of labor" without further criticism, and then simply asked the question, How is this price determined? It soon recognized that the change in the relations of demand and supply explained in regard to the price of labor, as of all other commodities, nothing except its changes, i.e., the oscillations of the market price above or below a certain mean.—C. 1.

PRIESTS
The priests are the most clever people.—Ltr. to Engels.

PRIMITIVE ACCUMULATION
The so-called primitive accumulation is nothing else than the historical process of divorcing the producer from the means of production. It appears as primitive, because it forms the prehistoric stage of capital and of the mode of production corresponding with it.—C. 1.

PRIMITIVE SOCIETY
Village communities were found to have been the primitive form of society.—C. M.

PRIMORDIAL CONDITION
Do not let us go back to a fictitious primordial condition as the political economist does, when he tries to explain. Such a primordial condition explains nothing. He merely pushes the question away into a gray nebulous distance. He assumes in the form of fact, of an event, what he is supposed to deduce—namely, the necessary relationship between two things—between, for example, division of labor and exchange.—M.

PRINCIPLE
Each principle has had its century in which to manifest itself.—P. P.

PRIVATE PROPERTY
(Private) property relations are the condition for the existence of the bourgeoisie and of its rule.—C. M.

Private property rests altogether on partitioning.—M.

You are horrified at our intending to do away with private property. But in your existing society, private property is already done away with for nine-tenths of the population; its existence for the few is solely due to its non-existence in the hands of those nine-tenths. You reproach us, therefore, with intending to do away with a form of property, the necessary condition for whose existence is, the non-existence of any property for the immense majority of society.—C. M.

The serf is the adjunct of the land. Likewise, the lord of an entailed estate, the first-born son, belongs to the land. It inherits him. Indeed, the dominion of private property begins with property in land—that is its basis.—M.

PRODUCTION, AIM OF

The directing motive, the end and aim of capitalist production, is to extract the greatest possible amount of surplus-value, and consequently to exploit labor-power to the greatest possible extent.—C. 1.

PRODUCTION, REVOLUTIONIZING OF

Suppose a shoemaker, with given tools, makes in one working day of twelve hours one pair of boots. If he must make two pairs in the same time, the productiveness of his labor must be doubled; and this cannot be done, except by an alteration in his tools or in his mode of working, or in both. Hence, the conditions of production, i.e., his mode of production, and the labor-process itself, must be revolutionized.—C. 1.

PRODUCTION, SPHERES OF

One sphere of production is, in fact, just as good or just as bad as another. Every one of them yields the same profit, and every one of them would be useless if the commodities it produced did not satisfy some social need.—C. 3.

PRODUCTION TIME

It is important to insist upon the point, that what determines value is not the time in which a thing has been produced, but the minimum time in which it is susceptible of being produced, and this minimum is demonstrated by competition.—P. P.

PRODUCTIVE ACTIVITY

Productive activity is nothing but the expenditure of human labor power. Tailoring and weaving, though qualitatively different productive activities, are each a productive expenditure of human brains, nerves, and muscles, and in this sense are human labor. They are but two different modes of expending human labor power. Of course, this labor power, which remains the same under all its modifications, must have attained a certain pitch of development before it can be expended in a multiplicity of modes.—C. 1.

PRODUCTIVE CAPITAL

Productive capital, in performing its functions, consumes its own component parts for the purpose of transforming them into a mass of products of a higher value.—C. 2.

PRODUCTIVE CONSUMPTION

In reality, the individual consumption of the laborer is unproductive as regards himself, for it produces nothing but the needy individual; it is productive to the capitalist and the state, since it is the production of the power that creates their wealth.—C. 1.

PRODUCTIVE LABOR

When we speak of productive labor, we speak of socially determined labor, labor which implies a quite specific relation between the buyer and the seller of the labor.—C. 4.

The first reason why Adam Smith calls this kind of labor "productive" is that the physiocrats call it "unproductive" and "nonproductive."—C. 4.

A productive laborer is one whose labor produces commodities; and indeed such a laborer does not consume more commodities than he produces, than his labor costs. His labor fixes and realizes itself "in some such vendible commodity," "in any vendible commodity which can replace the value of their wages and maintenance."—C. 4.

The aim of the capitalist production process is the accumulation of wealth, the self-expansion of value, its increase; that is to say, the maintenance of the old value and the creation of surplus-value. And it achieves this specific product of the capitalist production process only in exchange with labor, which for that reason is called *productive labor.*—C. 4.

Only bourgeois narrow-mindedness, which regards the capitalist forms of production as absolute forms—hence as eternal, natural forms of production—can confuse the question of what is productive labor from the standpoint of capital with the question of what labor is productive in general, or what is *productive labor* in general; and consequently fancy itself very wise in giving the answer that all labor which produces anything at all, which has any kind of result, is by that very fact productive labor.—C. 4.

PROLETARIAT

The proletariat will use its political supremacy to wrest, by degrees, all capital from the bourgeoisie, to centralize all instruments of production in the hands of the state, i.e., of the proletariat organized as the ruling class; and to increase the total of productive forces as rapidly as possible.—C. M.

Since the *proletariat* must first of all acquire political supremacy, must rise to be the leading class of the nation, must constitute itself the nation, it is, so far, itself national, though not in the bourgeois sense of the word.—C. M.

By proletariat is meant the class of modern wage-laborers who, having no means of production of their own, are reduced to selling their labor power in order to live.—C. M.

Accumulation of capital is increase of the proletariat.—C. 1.

With the development of industry the proletariat not only increases in number, it becomes concentrated in great masses, its strength grows, and it feels that strength more. The various interests and conditions of life within the ranks of the proletariat are more and more equalized.—C. M.

The proletariat is recruited from all classes of the population. —C. M.

Not only has the bourgeoisie forged the weapons that bring death to itself; it has also called into existence the men who are to wield those weapons—the modern working class—the proletarians. In proportion as the bourgeoisie, i.e., capital, is developed, in the same proportion is the proletariat, the modern working class, developed, a class of laborers, who live only so long as they find work, and who find work only so long as their labor increases capital.—C. M.

The proletarian is without property; his relation to his wife and children has no longer anything in common with the bourgeois family-relations; modern industrial labor, modern subjugation to capital, the same in England as in France, in America as in Germany, has stripped him of every trace of national character.—C. M.

By heralding the dissolution of the hereto existing world order the proletariat merely proclaims the secret of its own existence for it is the factual dissolution of that world order. By demanding the negation of private property, the proletariat merely raises to the rank of a principle of society what society has raised to the rank of its principle, what is already incorporated in it as the negative result of society without its own participation.—C. C.

The proletariat cannot be abolished without philosophy being made a reality.—C. C.

PROLETARIAT, GERMAN

The proletariat is beginning to appear in Germany as a result of the rising industrial movement. For it is not the naturally arising poor but the artificially impoverished, not the human masses mechanically oppressed by the gravity of society but the masses resulting from the drastic dissolution of society mainly of the middle class, that form the proletariat.—C. C.

PROMETHEUS

Prometheus is the noblest of saints and martyrs in the calendar of philosophy.—D. E.

PROOF

Any anticipation of results still to be proved appears to me to be disturbing.—P. E.

PROPERTY

Society itself is the root of property.—C. 4.

Are not most of your court proceedings concerned with property?—L. A.

The capitalist gains by virtue of the favorable situation of his *property.*—M.

The separation of property from labor has become the necessary consequence of a law that apparently originated in their identity.—C. 1.

R

RADICALISM
To be radical is to grasp the root of the matter. But for man the root is man himself.—C. C.

RAILWAYS
The emergence of railways in the leading capitalist countries permitted these nations to enlarge their capitalistic superstructure out of proportion to the production at large.—Ltr. to Danielson.

The railways usually hastened immensely the development of foreign commerce.—Ltr. to Danielson.

Originally in the construction of modern railways it was the prevailing opinion, pursued by the most prominent practical engineers, that a railway would last a century and that the wear and tear of the rails was so imperceptible that it could be ignored for all financial and other practical purposes. But it was soon found that the life of a rail did not exceed an average of 20 years.—C. 2.

RATE AND MASS OF SURPLUS-VALUE

It is to be emphasized that with a capital of a given magnitude the rate of surplus-value may rise, while its mass is decreasing, and vice versa. The mass of surplus-value is equal to the rate multiplied by the number of laborers; however, the rate is never calculated on the total, but only on the variable capital, actually only for every working day. On the other hand, with a given magnitude of capital-value, the rate of profit can neither rise nor fall without the mass of surplus-value also rising or falling.— C. 3.

RATE OF EXCHANGE

The rate of exchange is known to be the barometer for the international movement of money metals. If England has more payments to make to Germany than Germany to England, the price of marks, expressed in sterling, rises in London, and the price of sterling, expressed in marks, falls in Hamburg and Berlin. If this preponderance of England's payment obligations toward Germany is not balanced again, for instance, by a preponderance of purchases by Germany in England, the sterling price of bills of exchange in marks on Germany must rise to the point where it will pay to send metal (gold bullion) from England to Germany in payment of obligations, instead of sending bills of exchange. This is the typical course of events.—C. 3.

RATE OF PROFIT

The rate of profit is the motive power of capitalist production. Things are produced only so long as they can be produced with a profit. Hence the concern of the English economists over the decline of the rate of profit. The fact that the bare possibility of this happening should worry Ricardo, shows his profound understanding of the condition of capitalist production. It is that which is held against him, it is his unconcern about "human beings," and his having an eye solely for the development of the productive forces—it is precisely that which is the important thing about him.—C. 3.

Given the *rate of profit*, the absolute increase in the mass of capital depends on its existing magnitude. On the other hand, if its magnitude is given, the proportion of its growth, i.e., the rate of its increment, depends on the rate of profit.—C. 3.

RAW MATERIAL

The rate of profit depends partly on the good quality of the raw material. Good material produces less waste. Less raw materials are then needed to absorb the same quantity of labor. The laborer needs more time when using bad raw materials to process the same quantity.—C. 3.

If the subject of labor has, so to say, been filtered through previous labor, we call it raw material; such is ore already extracted and ready for washing. All raw material is the subject of labor, but not every subject of labor is raw material; it can only become so, after it has undergone some alteration by means of labor.—C. 1.

RAW PRODUCE

The greater demand for raw produce, and therefore the rise in value, may in part result from the increase of population and from the increase of their needs.—M.

In the manufacture of locomotives, every day the waste amounts to whole wagonloads of iron filings. These are collected and resold (or charged in account) to the same iron manufacturer who supplied the locomotive manufacturer with his principal *raw material*. The iron manufacturer again gives them solid form, adding new labor to them. However, in the form in which he sends them back to the locomotive manufacturer, these filings represent the part of the value of the product which replaces raw material. In this way not the same filings, but constantly a certain quantity of filings, move hither and thither between the two factories. This part forms in turn the raw material for each of the two branches of industry and, considered as value, only wanders from one shop to the other.—C. 4.

The *raw material* serves merely as an absorbent of a definite quantity of labor. By this absorption it is in fact changed into (a product) .—C. 1.

REASON
Human reason, which is nothing less than pure, having only an incomplete view, meets at each step fresh problems to solve.—P. P.

If you base yourself on giving to Caesar the things which are Caesar's and to God the things which are God's, do not consider the mammon of gold alone but at least just as much free reason as the Caesar of this world.—L. A.

In capitalist society social reason always asserts itself only post festum.—C. 2.

REPAIRMEN
There is a numerically unimportant class of persons, whose occupation it is to look after the whole of the machinery and repair it from time to time; such as engineers, mechanics, joiners, etc. This is a superior class of workmen, some of them scientifically educated, others brought up in the trade;

it is distinct from the factory operative class, and merely ag-gregated to it.—C. 1.

REPRODUCTION
No society can go on producing, in other words, no society can reproduce, unless it constantly reconverts a part of its products into means of production, or elements of fresh products.—C. 1.

REPRODUCTION OF CAPITAL
The maintenance and reproduction of the working class is, and must ever be, a necessary condition to the reproduction of capital. But the capitalist may safely leave its fulfillment to the laborer's instincts of self-preservation and of propa-gation. All the capitalist cares for is to reduce the laborer's individual consumption as far as possible to what is strictly necessary.—C. 1.

REPULSION AND ATTRACTION OF CAPITAL
The splitting up of the total social capital into many indi-vidual capitals or the repulsion of its fractions one from an-other is counteracted by their attraction.—C. 1.

RESEARCH
Research must never appeal to the powers of comprehen-sion of the masses, i.e., must never become popular and clear to itself.—L. A.

RESEARCH, SCIENTIFIC
Who should decide on the bounds of scientific research if not scientific research itself!—L. A.

RESISTANCE TO CAPITALIST DOMINATION
As the number of cooperating laborers increases, so too

does their resistance to the domination of capital, and with it, the necessity for capital to overcome this resistance by counter-pressure.—C. 1.

RESOLUTENESS, COMMUNIST
The communists are the most resolute section of the working class parties of every country, that section which pushes forward all others.—C. M.

RESPECTABILITY, CAPITALIST
Only as personified capital is the capitalist respectable.—C. 1.

RESTRICTION
All fetters and *restrictions* placed on manufacturers and foreign trade make manufactured commodities, etc., dearer.—C. 4.

RETAIL BUSINESS
Retail business deals with direct consumption.—C. 3.

RETRIBUTION
It is a rule of historical retribution that its instrument be forged not by the offended, but by the offender himself.—D. T.

REVIEWER
The uninformed reviewer tries to hide his complete ignorance and intellectual poverty by hurling the "utopian phrase" at the positive critic's head.—M.

REVOLT
Along with the constantly diminishing number of the magnates of capital, who usurp and monopolize all advantages of this process of transformation, grows the mass of misery, oppression, slavery, degradation, exploitation; but with this

too grows the *revolt of the working class*, a class always increasing in numbers, and disciplined, united, organized by the very mechanism of the process of capitalist production itself.—C. 1.

REVOLUTION
Revolutionary upheavals periodically recur in history.—C. 1.

The already existing conditions of life of the various generations also decide whether the revolutionary upheavals that periodically recur in history are strong enough to overthrow the basis of all that is in existence; if these material elements of a complete overthrow, to wit, on one side the existing production forces and on the other the formation of a revolutionary mass which revolts not only against individual conditions of hitherto existing society but against the very "life-production" hitherto existing, the "whole of the activity" on which it is based—if these material elements are not to hand it is absolutely indifferent for practical development, as the history of communism proves, whether the *idea* of that revolution has already been formulated a hundred times.—G. I.

REVOLUTION, BOURGEOIS
The bourgeoisie cannot exist without constantly revolutionizing the instruments of production, and thereby the relations of production, and with them the whole relations of society. Conservation of the old modes of production in unaltered form was, on the contrary, the first condition of existence for earlier industrial classes. Constant revolutionizing of production, uninterrupted disturbance of all social conditions, everlasting uncertainty and agitation distinguish the bourgeois epoch from earlier ones. All fixed, fast-frozen relations, with their train of ancient and venerable preju-

dices and opinions, are swept away, all newly formed ones become antiquated before they can ossify. All that is solid melts into air, all that is holy is profaned, and man is at last compelled to face with sober senses his real conditions of life.—C. M.

REVOLUTION, COMMUNIST
The communist revolution is the most radical rupture with traditional property relations; no wonder that its development involves the most radical rupture with traditional ideas.—C. M.

REVOLUTION, COURSE OF
In the beginning, the (revolutionary) measures appear economically insufficient and untenable, but, in the course of the movement, they outstrip themselves.—C. M.

REVOLUTION, FUTURE
Doctrinaire and utopian predictions about the future revolution only divert us from the reality of the present class struggle.—Ltr. to Nieuwenhuis.

Eventually wages, which have already been reduced to a minimum, must be reduced yet further, to meet the new competition. This then necessarily leads to revolution.—M.

REVOLUTION, PROLETARIAN
The scientific observation of the disintegrating bourgeois society guarantees sufficiently the assumption that after the outbreak of the proletarian revolution the conditions for its next actions will be available.—Ltr. to Nieuwenhuis.

Bourgeois revolutions rush onward rapidly from success to success, their stage effects outbid one another, men and things seem to be set in flaming brilliants, ecstasy is the prevailing spirit; but they are short-lived, they reach their climax speedily, then society relapses into a long fit of nervous reaction before it learns how to appropriate the fruits of its period of feverish excitement. *Proletarian* revolutions, on the contrary, criticize themselves constantly; constantly interrupt themselves in their own course; come back to what seems to have been accomplished, in order to start over anew; scorn with cruel thoroughness the half measures, weaknesses and meannesses of their first attempts.—E. B.

REVOLUTION, SOCIAL
From forms of development of the productive forces the property relations turn into their fetters. Then begins an epoch of social revolution.—P. E.

REVOLUTIONARY CLASS
Of all the classes that stand face to face with the bourgeoisie today, the proletariat alone is a really revolutionary class.—C. M.

The revolutionary (proletarian) class holds the future in its hands.—C. M.

REVOLUTIONARY IDEAS
When people speak of ideas that revolutionize society, they do but express the fact, that within the old society the elements of a new one have been created, and that the dissolution of the old ideas keeps even pace with the dissolution of the old conditions of existence.—C. M.

REVOLUTIONARY MOVEMENT
That the entire revolutionary movement necessarily finds both its empirical and its theoretical basis in the movement

of private property—in that of economy, to be precise—is easy to see.—M.

RICARDO

Ricardo, the creator of modern political economy in Great Britain, was convinced that political economy had nothing to do with questions of right (but of fact).—I. Q.

Ricardo's care for accumulation is even greater than his care for net profit, which he regards with fervent admiration as a means to accumulation. Hence too his contradictory admonitions and consoling remarks to the laborers. They are the people most interested in the accumulation of capital, because it is on this that the demand for them depends. If this demand rises, then the price of labor rises. They must therefore themselves desire the lowering of wages, so that the surplus taken from them, once more filtered through capital, is returned to them for new labor and their wages rise. This rise in wages however is bad, because it restricts accumulation. On the one hand they must not produce children. This brings a fall in the supply of labor, and so its price rises. But this rise diminishes the rate of accumulation, and so diminishes the demand for them and brings down the price of labor. Even quicker than the supply of them falls, capital falls along with it. If they produce children, then they increase their own supply and reduce the price of labor; thus the rate of profit rises, and with it the accumulation of capital. But the laboring population must rise in the same degree as the accumulation of capital; that is to say, the laboring population must be there exactly in the numbers that the capitalist needs—which it does anyway.—C. 4.

RICHES

A country is the richer the smaller its productive population is *relatively* to the total product; just as for the individual capitalist: the fewer laborers he needs to produce the same surplus, so much the better for him. The country is the richer the smaller the productive population in relation to the unproductive, the quantity of products remaining the same. For the relative smallness of the productive population would be only another way of expressing the relative degree of the productivity of labor.—C. 4.

ROBOT, THE WORKER AS
With the division of labor on one hand and the accumulation of capital on the other, the worker becomes ever more exclusively dependent on labor, and on a particular, very one-sided machine-like labor. He is thus depressed spiritually and physically to the condition of a machine and from being a man becomes an abstract activity and a stomach.—M.

ROMAN RELIGION
Epicurean, stoic or skeptic philosophy was the religion of the Romans of culture when Rome reached the zenith of its career.—L. A.

ROMANTICISM
Romanticism appears more and more as the "presupposition" of the critical criticism.—Ltr. to Engels.

RUINOUS COMPETITION
The bigger capitalist can even bear temporary losses until the smaller capitalist is ruined and he finds himself freed from this competition.—M.

RULE OF LANDED PROPERTY
The rule of landed property does not appear directly as the rule of mere capital. For those belonging to it, the estate is

more like their fatherland. It is a constricted sort of nationality.—M.

RUSSIA
All strata of the Russian society are in a state of economic, moral and intellectual disintegration.—Ltr. to Sorge.

The movement is progressing in Russia faster than in all the rest of Europe.—Ltr. to Engels.

Russia will be so kind as to participate in the next revolution.—Ltr. to Engels.

RUSSIAN LANDOWNERS
As a result of the so-called emancipation of the peasants, the Russian landowners are now compelled to carry on agriculture with the help of wage-laborers instead of the forced labor of serfs.—C. 2.

S

SACRIFICE, PROLETARIAN
The raising of wages gives rise to overwork among the workers. The more they wish to earn, the more must they sacrifice their time and carry out slave-labor, in the service of avarice completely losing all their freedom, thereby they shorten their lives. This shortening of their life span is a favorable circumstance for the working class as a whole, for as a result of it an ever-fresh supply of labor becomes necessary. This class has always to sacrifice a part of itself in order not to be wholly destroyed.—M.

SATISFACTION, MODE OF
An object satisfies the wants directly as a means of subsistence, or indirectly as a means of production.—C. 1.

SAVING
Accumulate, accumulate! That is Moses and the prophets! "Industry furnishes the material which saving accumulates." Therefore, save, save, i.e., reconvert the greatest possible portion of surplus-value, or surplus-product into capital!—C. 1.

The less you eat, drink and read books; the less you think, love, theorize, sing, paint, fence, etc., the more you save— the greater becomes your treasure which neither moths nor dust will devour—your capital.—M.

SCARCITY
The greater the scarcity of the products offered relative to the demand, the dearer they are.—P. P.

SELLING AND BUYING
If selling and buying disappear, free selling and buying disappear also.—C. M.

SENSE PERCEPTION
Sense perception must be the basis of all science. Only when it proceeds from sense perception in the twofold form both of sensuous consciousness and of sensuous need— that is, only when science proceeds from nature—is it true science.—M.

SENSES
The forming of the five senses is a labor of the entire history of the world down to the present.—M.

Wherever the *sensuous affirmation* is the direct annulment of the object in its independent form (as in eating, drinking, working, etc.), this is the affirmation of the object.—M.

SENSUOUS WORLD
The more the worker by his labor appropriates the external world, sensuous nature, the more he deprives himself of means of life in the double respect: first, that the sensuous external world more and more ceases to be an object belonging to his labor—to be his labor's means of life; and

secondly, that it more and more ceases to be means of life in the immediate sense, means for the physical subsistence of the worker.—M.

SEPARATION
Separation appears as the normal relation in this society. Where therefore it does not in fact apply, it is presumed and so far correctly; for in this society unity appears as accidental, separation as normal, and consequently separation is maintained as the relation even when one person unites separate functions.—C. 4.

SEPARATION OF CHURCH AND STATE
Was it not Christianity before anything else that separated church and state?—L. A.

SEPARATION OF LABORERS
The capitalist system presupposes the complete separation of the laborers from all property in the means by which they can realize their labor. As soon as capitalist production is once on its own legs, it not only maintains this separation, but reproduces it on a continually extending scale.—C. 1.

SERVICES
Services may also be forced on me—the services of officials, etc.—C. 4.

SERVICES, ENJOYMENT OF
Certain services, or the use-values, resulting from certain forms of activity or labor are embodied in commodities; others on the contrary leave no tangible result existing apart from the persons themselves who perform them; in other words, their result is not a vendible commodity. For example, the service a singer renders to me satisfies my aes-

thetic need; but what I enjoy exists only in an activity inseparable from the singer himself, and as soon as his labor, the
singing, is at an end, my enjoyment too is at an end. I enjoy
the activity itself—its reverberation on my ear.—C. 4.

SEXUAL RELATIONS
The direct, natural, and necessary relation of person to person is the relation of man to woman. In this natural relationship of the sexes man's relation to nature is
immediately his relation to man, just as his relation to man
is immediately his relation to nature—his own natural function. In this relationship, therefore, is sensuously manifested, reducible to an observable fact, the extent to which
the human essence has become nature to man, or to which
nature has to him become the human essence of man.—M.

In the approach to woman as the spoil and handmaid of
communal lust, is expressed the infinite degradation in
which man exists for himself, for the secret of this approach
has its unambiguous, decisive, plain and undisguised expression in the relation of man to woman and in the manner
in which the direct and natural procreative relationship is
conceived.—M.

Mill suggests public acclaim for those who prove themselves continent in their sexual relations.—M.

SHAKESPEARE
In *Timon of Athens*, Shakespeare excellently depicts the real
nature of money.—M.

SHORTENING OF LABOR-TIME
The shortening of the working day is by no means what is
aimed at, in capitalist production, when labor is econo-

mized by increasing its productiveness. It is only the shortening of the labor-time necessary for the production of a definite quantity of commodities that is aimed at.—C. 1.

SIGHT
The light from an object is perceived by us not as the subjective excitation of our optic nerve, but as the objective form of something outside the eye itself. But, in the act of seeing, there is at all events an actual passage of light from one thing to another, from the external object to the eye.—C.

SIMPLE REPRODUCTION
In the case of simple reproduction the surplus-value produced and realized annually, or periodically, if there are several turnovers during the year, is consumed individually, that is to say, unproductively, by its owner, the capitalist.—C. 2.

Apart from all accumulation, the mere continuity of the process of production, in other words, simple reproduction, sooner or later, and of necessity, converts every capital into accumulated capital, or capitalized surplus-value.—C. 1.

SKEPTICISM
The medical skepticism of the Parisian professors and students seems to be the order of the day.—Ltr. to Engels.

SLAVE CLASS
The worker gets the smallest and utterly indispensable part of the whole produce—as much, only, as is necessary for the propagation, not of humanity, but of the slave class of workers.—M.

SLAVE DEALER

The capitalist buys children and young persons under age. Previously, the workman sold his own labor power, which he disposed of nominally as a free agent. Now he sells wife and child. He has become a slave dealer.—C. 1.

SLAVE MARKET

The slave market maintains its supply of the commodity labor power by war, piracy, etc., and this rapine is not promoted by a process of circulation, but by the actual appropriation of the labor power of others by direct physical compulsion. Even in the United States, after the conversion of the buffer territory between the wage-labor states of the North and the slavery states of the South into a slave-breeding region for the South, where the slave thrown on the market thus became himself an element of the annual reproduction, this did not suffice for a long time, so that the African slave trade was continued as long as possible to satisfy the market.—C. 2.

SLAVERY

Slavery is an economic category as well as any other.—P. P.

Man has often made man himself, under the form of slaves, serve as the primitive material of money.—C. 1.

The purchase and sale of slaves is formally also a purchase and sale of commodities. But money cannot perform this function without the existence of slavery. If slavery exists, then money can be invested in the purchase of slaves. On the other hand, the mere possession of money cannot make slavery possible.—C. 2.

SLAVERY, BOURGEOIS

Direct slavery is the pivot of bourgeois industry as well as machinery, credit, etc. Without slavery you have no cotton, without cotton you cannot have modern industry. It is slavery which has given their value to the colonies, it is the colonies which have created the commerce in the world, it is the commerce of the world which is the essential condition of the great industry. Thus slavery is an economic category of the highest importance.—P. P.

SLUMP

Whilst labor brings about the accumulation of capitals and with this the increasing prosperity of society, it renders the worker ever more dependent on the capitalist, leads him into competition of a new intensity, and drives him into the headlong rush of overproduction, with the subsequent corresponding slump.—M.

SMALL CAPITALIST

It is obvious that where industrial labor has reached a high level, and where therefore almost all manual labor has become factory-labor, the entire capital of a small capitalist does not suffice to provide him even with the necessary fixed capital.—M.

The small capitalist has the choice: (1) either to consume his capital, since he can no longer live on the interest—and thus cease to be a capitalist; or (2) to set up a business himself, sell his commodity cheaper, buy dearer than the wealthier capitalist, and pay increased wages—thus ruining himself, the market-price being already very low as a result of the intense competition presupposed.—M.

SMALL PROPERTY

While every social improvement benefits the big estate, it harms small property, because it increases its need for ready cash.—M.

SMITH, ADAM

Adam Smith, like all economists worth speaking of, takes over from the physiocrats the conception of the average wage, which he calls the natural price of wages.—C. 4.

Adam Smith discovered the division of labor.—P. P.

Engels was right to call Adam Smith the Luther of political economy.—M.

Adam Smith very acutely notes that the really great development of the productive power of labor starts only from the moment when it is transformed into wage-labor, and the conditions of labor confront it on the one hand as landed property and on the other as capital.—C. 4.

The capitalist, Adam Smith says, "could have no interest to employ the laborers, unless he expected from the sale of their work something more than what was sufficient to replace his stock to him."—C. 4.

Adam Smith's contradictions are of significance because they contain problems which it is true he does not solve, but which he reveals by contradicting himself. His correct insistence in this connection is best shown by the fact that his successors take opposing stands based on one aspect of his teaching or the other.—C. 4.

Adam's twistings and turnings, his contradictions and wanderings from the point, prove that, once he had made wages, profit and rent the constituent component parts of exchangeable value or of the total price of the market, he had got himself stuck in the mud and had to get stuck.—C. 4.

SOCIAL CONSCIOUSNESS
The social consciousness of past ages, despite all the multiplicity and variety it displays, moves within certain common forms, or general ideas, which cannot completely vanish except with the total disappearance of class antagonism.—C. M.

SOCIAL EVENTS
While every *social improvement* benefits the big estate, it harms small property.—M.

Man's reflections on the forms of *social life,* and consequently, also, his scientific analysis of those forms, take a course directly opposite to that of their actual historical development. He begins, post festum, with the results of the process of development ready to hand before him.—C. 1.

No *social order* ever perishes before all the productive forces for which there is room in it have developed; and new, higher relations of production never appear before the material conditions of their existence have matured in the womb of the old society.—P. E.

SOCIAL RANK
In the early epochs of history, we find almost everywhere a complicated arrangement of society into various orders, a manifold graduation of social rank. In ancient Rome we

have patricians, knights, plebeians, slaves; in the Middle Ages, feudal lords, vassals, guild-masters, journeymen, apprentices, serfs; in almost all of these classes, again, subordinate graduations.—C. M.

SOCIAL RELATIONS
In the social production of their life, men enter into definite relations that are indispensable and independent of their will.—P. E.

SOCIAL SCUM
The "dangerous class," the social scum, that passively rotting mass thrown off by the lowest layers of old society, may, here and there, be swept into the movement by a proletarian revolution; its conditions of life, however, prepare it far more for the part of a bribed tool of reactionary intrigue.—C. M.

SOCIALISM
A group of immature students and sophisticated doctors intend to install a "higher ideal" objective to socialism, replacing its materialistic foundation by present-day mythology, especially by the goddesses of Justice, Freedom, Equality and Fraternity.—Ltr. to Sorge.

Socialism is man's positive self-consciousness, no longer mediated through the annulment of religion, just as real life is man's positive reality, no longer mediated through the annulment of private property, through communism.—M.

We have seen what significance, given socialism, the wealth of human needs has, and what significance, therefore, both a new mode of production and a new object of production have: a new manifestation of the forces of human nature and a new enrichment of human nature. Under private property their significance is reversed: every person speculates on creating a new need in another, so as to drive him to a fresh sacrifice, to place him in a new dependence and to seduce him into a new mode of gratification and therefore economic ruin.—M.

It will be seen how in place of the wealth and poverty of political economy come the rich human being and the rich human need. The rich human being is simultaneously the human being in need of a totality of human life-activities—the man in whom his own realization exists as an inner necessity, as need. Not only wealth, but likewise the poverty of man—given socialism—receives in equal measure a human and therefore social significance.—M.

SOCIALISM, BOURGEOIS

A part of the bourgeoisie is desirous of redressing social grievances, in order to secure the continued existence of bourgeois society. To this section belong economists, philanthropists, humanitarians, improvers of the condition of the working class, organizers of charity, members of societies for the prevention of cruelty to animals, temperance, fanatics, hole and corner reformers of every imaginable kind. This form of socialism has, moreover, been worked out into complete systems.—C. M.

The socialistic bourgeois want all the advantages of modern social conditions without the struggles and dangers necessarily resulting therefrom. They desire the existing state of society minus its revolutionary and disintegrating elements. They wish for a bourgeoisie without a proletariat.—C. M.

A more practical, but less systematic, form of bourgeois socialism sought to depreciate every revolutionary movement in the eyes of the working class, by showing that no mere political reform, but only a change in the material conditions of existence in economic relations, could be of any advantage to them.—C. M.

In countries like France, where the peasants constitute far more than half of the population, it was natural that writers who sided with the proletariat against the bourgeoisie, should use, in their criticism of the bourgeois regime, the standard of the peasant and petty bourgeois, and from the standpoint of these intermediate classes should take up the cudgels for the working class. Thus arose the petty bourgeois socialism.—C. M.

SOCIALISM, CLERICAL
As the parson has ever gone hand in hand with the landlord, so has Clerical Socialism with Feudal Socialism.—C. M.

SOCIALISM, FEUDAL
Feudal socialism arose: half lamentation, half lampoon; half echo of the past, half menace of the future; at times, by its bitter, witty and incisive criticism, striking the bourgeoisie to the very heart's core, but always ludicrous in its effect, through total incapacity to comprehend the march of modern history.—C. M.

SOCIALISM, GERMAN
While this "true" (German) socialism thus served the government as a weapon for fighting the German bourgeoisie, it, at the same time, directly represented a reactionary interest, the interest of the German philistines.—C. M.

SOCIALISM, UTOPIAN

The utopian socialists reject all political, and especially all revolutionary, action; they wish to attain their ends by peaceful means, and endeavor, by small experiments, necessarily doomed to failure, and by the force of example, to pave the way for the new social Gospel.—C. M.

These proposals are of a purely utopian character. The significance of critical-utopian socialism and communism bears an inverse relation to historical development. In proportion as the modern class struggle develops and takes definite shape, this fantastic standing apart from the contest, these fantastic attacks on it lose all practical value and all theoretical justification. —C. M.

SOCIALIST GOVERNMENT

A socialist government can only gain power in a country when conditions are so that it can intimidate the bourgeoisie sufficiently.—Ltr. to Nieuwenhuis.

SOCIALIST MAN

Since for socialist man the entire so-called history of the world is nothing but the begetting of man through human labor, nothing but the coming-to-be of nature of man, he has the visible, irrefutable proof of his birth through himself, of his process of coming-to-be.—M.

SOCIALISTS

As the economists are the scientific representatives of the bourgeois class, so the socialists and communists are the theorists of the proletarian class.—P. P.

SPECULATION

At a certain high point the increasing concentration of capital in its turn causes a new fall in the rate of profit. The mass of small dispersed capitals is thereby driven along the adventurous road of speculation, credit frauds, stock swindles, and crises.—C. 3.

SPINNING MACHINE
A spinning machine has no use-value unless it is used for spinning, unless therefore it functions as a fixed component part of a productive capital. But a spinning machine is movable. It may be exported from the country in which it was produced and sold abroad directly or indirectly for raw materials, etc., or for champagne.—C. 2.

SPIRITUAL SUPERSTRUCTURE (UEBERBAU)
From the specific form of material production arises in the first place a specific (ideological super-) structure of society, in the second place a specific relation of men to nature. Their state and their spiritual outlook is determined by both. Therefore also the kind of their spiritual production.—C. 4.

SPONTANEOUS ACTIVITY
The worker's activity is not his spontaneous activity. It belongs to another; it is the loss of his self.—M.

Generatio aequivoca (*spontaneous generation*) is the only practical refutation of the theory of creation.—M.

STAGNANT SURPLUS POPULATION
The stagnant surplus population is characterized by maximum of working time, and minimum of wages.—C. 1.

STATE
Political economy in its classical period, like the bourgeoisie

itself in its parvenu period, adopted a severely critical atti-
tude to the machinery of the state, etc. At a later stage it realized and—as was shown too in practice—learnt from
experience that the necessity for the inherited social combination of all these classes, which in part were totally unproductive, arose from its own organization.—C. 4.

The state is only justified insofar as it is a committee to administer the common interests of the productive bourgeoisie.—M.

In the *state,* where man counts merely as one of his kind, he
is an imaginary link in an imagined chain of sovereignty,
robbed of his individual life and endowed with an unreal
generality.—J. Q.

STATE, BOURGEOIS
The perfect political state by its nature defines the life of
man as of a particular kind, in opposition to his material
life. In bourgeois society all the assumptions of this self-
centered material life remain outside the sphere of the
state.—J. Q.

STATE, CHRISTIAN
The so-called Christian state is a Christian denial of the
state, not in any way the political fulfillment of Christianity.
The state that continues to profess Christianity as a religion
does not yet profess it in political form because it still be-
haves religiously toward religion. This means that it is not a
genuine fulfillment of the human basis of religion, because
it is still the product of unreality, of the imaginary shape of
the human nucleus. The so-called Christian state is the im-
perfect state, and it treats Christianity as a supplementation

and sanctification of its imperfection. It treats religion as a means to an end and becomes thereby hypocritical.—J. Q.

STATE, MODERN
Whereas the earlier teachers of state law construed the state out of ambition or sociability, or even reason, though not out of the reason of society but rather out of the reason of the individual, the more ideal and profound view of modern philosophy construes it out of the idea of the whole.—L. A.

STATE, RELIGIOUS
The truly religious state is the theocratic state.—L. A.

STATE AND RELIGION
Once the state includes several confessions with equal rights it cannot be a religious state without violating particular confessions; it cannot be a church which condemns adherents of another confession as heretics, which makes every piece of bread dependent on faith, which makes dogma the link between separate individuals and existence as citizens of the state.—L. A.

The point here is not whether the state should be philosophized about, but whether it should be philosophized about well or badly, philosophically or unphilosophically, with prejudice or without, with consciousness or without, consistently or inconsistently, in a completely rational or half rational way. If you make religion a theory of state right, then you make religion itself a kind of philosophy.—L. A.

STATISTICS
Statistics is not able to make actual analyses of the rates of wages in different epochs and countries, until the condi-

tions which shape the rate of profit are thoroughly understood. The rate of profit does not fall because labor becomes less productive, but because it becomes more productive. Both the rise in the rate of surplus-value and the fall in the rate of profit are but specific forms through which growing productivity of labor is expressed under capitalism.—C. 3.

STEAM
Steam and machinery revolutionized industrial production.—C. M.

STEEL RAILS
About 1867 began the introduction of *steel rails,* which cost about twice as much as iron rails but which last more than twice as long.—C. 2.

STIMULATION OF DEMAND
Under private property, every person speculates on creating a new need in another, so as to place him in a new dependence.—M.

STOCK EXCHANGE
Now you are a member of the stock exchange, and altogether respectable. My gratulations. I would like to hear you once howl among these wolves.—Ltr. to Engels.

STOCKS
Stock is called capital only when it yields to its owner a revenue or profit.—M.

SUPPLY AND DEMAND
In a final analysis, supply and demand bring together pro-

duction and consumption, but production and consumption based upon individual exchanges.—P. P.

Supply and demand coincide when their mutual proportions are such that the mass of commodities of a definite line of production can be sold at their market-value, neither above nor below it. That is the first thing we hear.—C. 3.

The smaller the supply relatively to the demand, the higher the exchange-value or the price of the product rises.—P. P.

Supply and demand determine the market-price, and so does the market-price, and the market-value in the further analysis, determine supply and demand. This is obvious in the case of demand, since it moves in a direction opposite to prices, swelling when prices fall, and vice versa. But this is also true of supply. Because the prices of means of production incorporated in the offered commodities determine the demand for these means of production, and thus the supply of commodities whose supply embraces the demand for these means of production.—C. 3.

If supply and demand balance one another, they cease to explain anything, do not affect market-values, and therefore leave us so much more in the dark about the reasons why the market-value is expressed in just this sum of money and no other. It is evident that the real inner laws of capitalist production cannot be explained by the interaction of supply and demand, because these laws cannot be observed in their pure state, until supply and demand cease to act, i.e., are equated.—C. 3.

If the demand, and consequently the market-price, falls, capital may be withdrawn, thus causing supply to shrink.

Conversely, if the demand increases, and consequently the market-price rises above the market-value, this may lead to too much capital flowing into this line of production and production may swell to such an extent that the market price will even fall below the market-value.—C. 3.

T

TASKS

Mankind always sets itself only such tasks as it can solve; since, looking at the matter more closely, it will always be found that the task itself arises only when the material conditions for its solution already exist or are at least in the process of formation.—P. E.

TECHNOLOGY

Technology discloses man's mode of dealing with nature, the process of production by which he sustains his life, and thereby also lays bare the mode of formation of his social relations, and of the mental conceptions that flow from them.—C. 1.

THEOLOGIAN, CRITICAL

Even the critical theologian remains a theologian. Hence, either he had to start from certain presuppositions of philosophy accepted as authoritative; or if in the process of criticism and as a result of other people's discoveries doubts about these philosophical presuppositions have risen in him, he abandons them without vindication and in a cowardly fashion, abstracts from them showing his servile dependence on these presuppositions and his resentment at this dependence merely in a negative, unconscious and sophistical manner.—M.

Whenever discoveries (such as Feuerbach's) are made about the nature of his own philosophic presuppositions the critical theologian partly makes it appear as if he were the one who had accomplished this, producing that appearance by taking the results of these discoveries and, without being able to develop them, hurling them in the form of catch-phrases at writers still caught in the confines of philosophy; partly he even manages to acquire a sense of his own superiority to such discoveries by covertly asserting in a veiled, malicious and skeptical fashion elements of the Hegelian dialectic.—M.

To the theological critic it seems quite natural that everything has to be done by philosophy, so that he can chatter away about purity, resoluteness, and utterly critical criticism; and he fancies himself the true conqueror of philosophy.—M.

The critical theologian is either forever repeating assurances about the purity of his own criticism, or tries to make it seem as though all that was left for criticism to deal with now was some other immature form of criticism outside itself—say eighteenth-century criticism—and the backwardness of the masses, in order to divert the observer's attention as well as his own from the necessary task of settling accounts between criticism and its point of departure.—M.

THEOLOGY
Theology explains the origin of evil by the fall of man: that is, it assumes as a fact, in historical form, what has to be explained. —M.

The justice in history assigns to theology, ever philosophy's spot of infection, the role of portraying in itself the negative dissolution of philosophy—i.e., the process of its decay.—M.

THEOLOGY, PROTESTANT
There are conclusive proofs that the hatred of the Protestant theology for philosophers arises largely out of philosophy's tolerance toward the particular confession as such.—L. A.

THEORETIC NOTIONS
For the mass of human beings, i.e., for the proletariat, these theoretic notions do not exist and therefore do not need to be dissolved and if ever this mass has any such notions, e.g., religion, they have been dissolved long ago by circumstances.—G. I.

TRUTH
Is there not a universal human nature just as there is a universal nature of plants and heavenly bodies? Philosophy asks what is true, not what is acknowledged as such, what is true for *all* men, not what is true for individuals: philosophy's metaphysical truths do not know the boundaries of political geography: its political truths know too well where the "boundaries" begin to confuse the illusory horizon of a particular world and national outlooks with the true horizon of the human mind.—L. A.

TURKS
The courageous Turks have accelerated the revolutionary

explosion by inflicting great damage to the name of the Russian dynasty as well as to the Russian army and Russian finances.—Ltr. to Sorge.

TURNCOAT, BOURGEOIS

In times when the class struggle nears the decisive hour, the process of dissolution going on within the ruling class, in fact, within the whole range of old society, assumes such a violent, glaring character, that a small section of the ruling class cuts itself adrift, and joins the revolutionary class.—C. M.

TURNOVER OF CAPITAL

The turnover of the fixed component part of capital, and therefore also the time of turnover necessary for it, comprises several turnovers of the circulating constituents of capital. In the time during which the fixed capital turns over once, the circulating capital turns over several times.—C. 2.

TWO CLASSES

The final consequence is the abolishment of the distinction between capitalist and landowner, so that there remain altogether only two classes of the population—the working class and the class of the capitalists. This huckstering with landed property, the transformation of landed property into a commodity, constitutes the final overthow of the old and the final consummation of the money aristocracy.—M.

U

UNDERSTRUCTURE (*UNTERBAU*), MATERIAL

History does not end by dissolving itself in "self-consciousness" as "the spirit of the spirit," but there is present in it at every stage a material result, a sum of production forces.—G. I.

UNEMPLOYED

They stand at opposite poles—unemployed capital at one pole and unemployed worker population at the other.—C. 3.

Political economy does not recognize the unoccupied workers, the workman insofar as he happens to be outside this labor-relationship. The cheat-thief, swindler, beggar, and unemployed man; the starving, wretched and criminal workingman—these are figures who do not exist for political economy but only for other eyes, those of the doctor, the judge, the gravedigger and bum-bailiff, etc.; such figures are specters outside the domain of political economy.—M.

UNEMPLOYMENT

The whole form of the movement of modern industry depends upon the constant transformation of a part of the laboring population into unemployed or half-employed hands.—C. 1.

A glaring contradiction—there is a complaint of the want of hands, while at the same time many thousands are out of work, because the division of labor chains them to a particular branch of industry.—C. 1.

UNFITNESS, BOURGEOIS
The bourgeoisie is unfit any longer to be the ruling class in society, and to impose its conditions of existence upon society as an overriding law. It is unfit to rule, because it is incompetent to assure an existence to its slave within his slavery, because it cannot help letting him sink into a state that it has to feed him, instead of being fed by him. Society can no longer live under this bourgeoisie, in other words, its existence is no longer compatible with society.—C. M.

UNHAPPINESS
Since a society is not happy of which the greater part suffers—yet even the wealthiest state of society leads to the suffering of the majority—and since the economic system (and in general a society based on private property) leads to this wealthiest condition, it follows that the goal of the economic system is the unhappiness of society.—M.

UNION OF WORKERS
Now and then the workers are victorious, but only for a time. The real fruits of their battles lie, not in the immediate result, but in the ever expanding union of the workers. This union is helped on by the improved means of communication that are created by modern industry, and that place the workers of different localities in contact with one another. It

was just this contact that was needed to centralize the numerous local struggles, all of the same character, into one national struggle between classes.— C. M.

UNITED ACTION
United action, of the leading civilized countries at least, is one of the first conditions for the emancipation of the proletariat.— C. M.

UNITED STATES
The United States have now surpassed England in the rapidity of economic progress.—Ltr. to Danielson.

That the bourgeois society in the United States has not yet developed far enough to render the class struggle evident and understandable is most noticeably shown by C. H. Carey, the only American economist of repute.—Ltr. to Weydemeyer.

UNITED STATES AND RUSSIA
It is difficult to draw an analogy between the United States and Russia. In the former the governmental expenses decrease daily and the public debt diminishes yearly; in the latter public bankruptcy seems to be inevitable. The former has liberated itself from pure paper money, while the latter has nothing better than paper money. The former again, shows an unprecedented industrial development, while the latter reverts itself to the time of Louis XIV and Louis XV.— Ltr. to Danielson.

UNITED STATES RAILWAYS
The railways of the United States were presented by the government not only with land necessary for their construction, but also with large stretches of property adjoining

both sides of the tracks. The railways thus became great landowners, while the small immigrant farmers settled near them, so as to secure good transportation for their produce.—Ltr. to Danielson.

UNITY
The communist organization turns existing conditions into conditions of (centralized) unity.—G. I.

UNIVERSALITY OF MAN
The universality of man is in practice manifested precisely in the universality which makes all nature his inorganic body—both inasmuch as nature is (1) his direct means of life, and (2) the material, the object, and the instrument of his life activity.—M.

UNPAID LABOR
There is not one single atom of capitalist value that does not owe its existence to unpaid labor.—C. 1.

UNPRODUCTIVE LABOR
The largest part of society, that is to say the working class, must perform this kind of labor for itself; but it is only able to perform it when it has labored "productively." It can only cook meat for itself when it has produced a wage with which to pay for the meat; and it can only keep its furniture and dwellings clean, it can only polish its boots, when it has produced the value of furniture, house rent and boots. To this class of productive laborers itself, therefore, the labor which they perform for themselves appears as "unproductive labor." This unproductive labor never enables them to repeat the same unproductive labor a second time unless they have previously labored productively.—C. 4.

To the extent that capital conquers the whole of production, and therefore the home and petty form of industry—in short, industry intended for self-consumption, not producing commodities—disappears, it is clear that the *unproductive laborers*, those whose services are directly exchanged against revenue, will for the most part be performing only *personal* services, and only an inconsiderable part of them (like cooks, seamstresses, jobbing tailors and so on) will produce material use-values.—C. 4.

UNPRODUCTIVITY
How very unproductive, from the standpoint of capitalist production, the laborer is who indeed produces vendible commodities, but only to the amount equivalent to his own laborpower, and therefore produces no surplus-value for capital—can be seen from the passages in Ricardo saying that the very existence of such people is a nuisance. This is the theory and practice of capital.—C. 4.

Is it not a contradiction that the "violin maker, the organ builder, the music dealer, the mechanic, etc.," are productive, and the professions for which these labors are only "preparations" are unproductive?—C. 4.

UNSKILLED LABOR
A commodity may be the product of the most skilled labor, but its value, by equating it to the product of simple unskilled labor, represents a definite quality of the latter labor alone. The different proportions in which different sorts of labor are reduced to unskilled labor as their standards are established by a social process that goes on behind the backs of the producers, and, consequently, appear to be fixed by custom.—C. 1.

URBANIZATION, BOURGEOIS

The bourgeoisie has subjected the country to the rule of the towns. It has created enormous cities, has greatly increased the urban population as compared with the rural, and has thus rescued a considerable part of the population from the idiocy of rural life.—C. M.

USE

Use determines a thing's value.—M.

The use of products is determined by the social conditions in which the consumers are placed, and these conditions themselves rest on the antagonism of classes.—P. P.

USE-VALUE

Use-values become a reality only by use or consumption: they also constitute the substance of all wealth, whatever may be the social form of that wealth.—C. 1.

A commodity, such as iron, corn, or a diamond, is, so far as it is a material thing, a use-value, something useful. This property of a commodity is independent of the amount of labor required to appropriate its useful qualities.—C. 1.

USELESS POPULATION

Production of too many useful things produces too large a useless population.—M.

USURER

Hoarding necessarily appears along with money. But the professional hoarder does not become important until he is transformed into a usurer.—C. 3.

USURER'S CAPITAL

Interest-bearing capital, or, as we may call it in its antiquated form, usurer's capital, belongs together with its
twin brother, merchant's capital, to the antediluvian forms
of capital, which long precede the capitalist mode of production and are to be found in the most diverse economic
formations of society.—C. 3.

USURY

Usury centralizes money wealth where the means of production are dispersed. It does not alter the mode of production, but attaches itself firmly to it like a parasite and makes
it wretched. It sucks out its blood, enervates it and compels
reproduction to proceed under ever more pitiable conditions. Hence the popular hatred against usurers, which was
most pronounced in the ancient world where ownership of
means of production by the producer himself was at the
same time the basis for political status, the independence of
the citizen.—C. 3.

V

VALUE
Value is the cornerstone of the economic edifice.—P. P.

The transformation of values into prices of production serves to obscure the basis for determining value itself.—C. 3.

VALUE OF LABOR
In the expression "value of labor," the idea of value is not only completely obliterated, but actually reversed. It is an expression as imaginary as the value of the earth. These imaginary expressions, arise, however, from the relations of production themselves. They are categories for the phenomenal forms of essential relations.—C. 1.

VARIABLE CAPITAL
That part of capital, represented by laborpower, does, in the process of production, undergo an alteration of value. It both reproduces the equivalent of its own value, and also produces an excess, a surplus-value, which may itself vary, may be more or less according to circumstances. This part of capital is continually being transformed from a constant

into a variable magnitude. I therefore call it the variable part of capital or, shortly, variable capital.—C. 1.

VICE
The interest obtained from the vices of the ruined proletarians stands in inverse proportion to it. (Prostitution, drunkenness, the pawnbroker.)—M.

VILLAGE SYSTEM
Village communities were found to be, or to have been, the primitive form of society everywhere from India to Ireland. The inner organization of this primitive communistic society was laid bare, in its typical form, by Morgan's crowning discovery of the true nature of the gens and its relation to the tribe. With the dissolution of these primeval communities society begins to be differentiated into separate and finally antagonistic classes.—C. M.

The so-called village system gave to each of the small Hindu unions their independent organization and distinct life.—D. T.

VULGAR ECONOMICS
Vulgar economy actually does no more than interpret, systematize and defend in doctrinaire fashion the conceptions of the agents of bourgeois production who are entrapped in bourgeois production relations. It should not astonish us, then, that vulgar economy feels particularly at home in the estranged outward appearances of economic relations in which these prima facie absurd and perfect contradictions appear and that these relations seem the more self-evident the more their internal relations are concealed from it, although they are understandable to the popular mind. But

all science would be superfluous if the outward appearance and the essence of things directly coincided.—C. 3.

The vulgar economist does practically no more than translate the singular concepts of the capitalists, who are in the thrall of competition, into a seemingly more theoretical and generalized language, and attempt to substantiate the justice of those conceptions.—C. 3.

W

WAGE FLUCTUATION
The growing competition among the bourgeoisie, and the resulting commercial crisis, make the wages of the workers ever more fluctuating.—C. M.

WAGE-LABOR
The condition of capital is wage-labor. Wage-labor rests exclusively on competition between the laborers.—C. M.

The average price of wage-labor is the minimum wage, i.e., that quantum of the means of subsistence which is absolutely requisite to keep the laborer in bare existence as a laborer. What, therefore, the wage-laborer appropriates by means of his labor, merely suffices to prolong and reproduce a bare existence.—C. M.

WAGES
What are wages? They are the value of labor.—P. P.

Wages rise with the rising prices of the necessities of life.

Wage advances are the consequence, not the cause, of advances in the prices of commodities.—C. 2.

According to the dogma of the economists, wages rise in consequence of accumulation of capital.—C. 1.

A forcing up of wages (disregarding all other difficulties, including the fact that it would only be by force, too, that the higher wages, being an anomaly, could be maintained) would therefore be nothing but better payment for the slave, and would not conquer either for the worker or for labor their human status and dignity.—M.

WEALTH, SOURCE OF
The original sources of all wealth are the soil and the laborer.—C. 1.

WEALTH OF SOCIETY
The wealth of a society is the result of the accumulation of much labor, capital being accumulated labor; the result, therefore, of the fact that his products are being taken in ever-increasing degree from the hands of the worker, that to an increasing extent his own labor confronts him as another's property and that the means of his existence and his activity are increasingly concentrated in the hands of the capitalist.—M.

The actual *wealth of society*, and the possibility of constantly expanding its reproduction process, do not depend upon the duration of surplus-labor, but upon its productivity and the more or less copious conditions of production under which it is performed.—C. 3.

WEAR AND TEAR
Wear and tear is first of all a result of use . . . Wear and tear is furthermore caused by the action of natural forces.—C. 2.

WHIM, CAPITALIST
The demand on which the life of the worker depends, depends on the whim of the rich and the capitalists.—M.

WINDMILL
The windmill gives you society with the feudal lord; the steam mill, society with the industrial capitalist.—P. P.

WIVES, BOURGEOIS
The bourgeois sees in his wife a mere instrument of production.—C. M.

WOMAN LABOR
The less the skill and exertion of strength implied in manual labor, in other words, the more modern industry becomes developed, the more is the labor of men superseded by that of women.—C. M.

WOMEN
Women, even when gifted with understanding, are curious creatures.—Ltr. to Engels.

WORKING DAY
The working day is . . . not a constant, but a variable quantity.—C. 1.

Hence it is that in the history of capitalist production the determination of what is a working day presents itself as the result of a struggle, a struggle between collective capital, i.e., the class of capitalists, and collective labor, i.e., the working class.—C. 1.

The sum of the necessary labor and the surplus-labor, i.e., of the periods of time during which the workman replaces the value of his labor power, and produces the surplus-value, this sum constitutes the actual time during which he works, i.e., the working day.—C. 1.

WORKSHOP
The knowledge, the judgment, and the will, which, though in ever so small a degree, are practiced by the independent peasant or handicraftsman, in the same way as the savage makes the whole art of war consist in the exercise of his personal cunning— these faculties are now required only for the workshop as a whole.—C. 1.

WORLD LITERATURE
National one-sidedness and narrow-mindedness become more and more impossible, and from the numerous national and local literatures there arises a world literature.—C. M.

WORLD MARKET
Modern industry has established the world market, for which the discovery of America paved the way. This market has given an immense development to commerce, to navigation, to communication by land.—C. M.

The specific aim of bourgeois society is the establishment of a *world market,* at least principally, and of a production founded on the world market.—Ltr. to Engels.

Developing the material forces of production and creating an appropriate *world market* is the historical task of the capitalist mode of production.—C. 3.